PRAISE FOR *THE NEXT HALF CENTURY*

"This book marshals a range of detailed facts to paint a picture of a remarkable change in prosperity of people around the world that we should expect to see over the next 50 years."

— **James D. Hamilton,** Professor of Economics, University of California at San Diego

"Our expectations for the coming months and years will evolve from a nexus of trends in the shifting growth of the economy across sections of the United States and among second and third world countries, declining birth rates, the aging of the world's population internationally, and climate change. *The Next Half Century* is a fascinating, highly readable and optimistic guide to these trends."

— **Maxwell McCombs,** Retired Chair of the Journalism Department at the University of Texas at Austin, coauthor of *Setting the Agenda: Mass Media and Public Opinion*

"Alan Nevin's new book, *The Next Half Century*, presents an optimistic view of how the economies of third world countries will flourish as educational opportunities increase and birth rates decline, allowing women greater participation in the work force. Nevin backs up his thesis with well-researched data.

He also contends that these countries must embrace five additional elements including increasing living wage employment, improving youth education, achieving gender equality in the workplace, responding to the environmental crisis, and bringing child labor to an end."

— **Barbara Bry,** Chief Financial Officer, Blackbird Ventures and author

"Alan Nevin's book is a thoughtful analysis that describes what has been, and what will become as a result of the demography he explores. It is a breezy read, with humor and insight, and helps readers understand the dynamics affecting growth and change in many communities. The data are presented in a clear manner, interspersed with anecdotes and narratives that elevate the relationships that drive behavior. I recommend this book for readers who wish to learn and assess, in part, what has caused the current environment, settings and development."

— **Dr. Steve Altman,** Former President of three universities

"I loved this book! I can't remember learning so much vital information, all giving me much greater perspective on our nation and the world— both today and in the decades to come—all based on data and objective, experienced analysis."

— **David Aretha,** award-winning author

"This book takes today's statistics and trends, and projects them into the future. Considering factors such as births, family formation, quality of life, education, the economy, power sources, labor, governance and geography, it foresees the most likely
developments to come."

— **Herbert Lazerow,** Professor of Law, University of San Diego

"In the past few months, I have had the great pleasure of getting to know Mr. Alan Nevin and have become aware of his wealth of knowledge and experience as an economist and real estate expert. I have reviewed this book and found it extremely interesting and intriguing.

Particularly at this juncture with rapid and consequential major changes in the world orders, including social and cultural, environmental, and climatic actions causing economic and political tensions, this publication will be useful for readers seeking to understand upcoming transformations through the lens of an expert who has the know-how to analyze the current factors affecting the world's economic trajectory. It is my great honor and pleasure to endorse this highly enlightening and timely book."

— **Mitra Kanaani,** FAIA, Former Chair, Undergraduate Program, New School of Architecture and Design

"For decades, Alan Nevin has taught, spoken, and written about San Diego rental housing's unique benefits. Millionaire investors, limited partners, developers, and professional students have benefited by discovering the economic and political tsunamis which have generated dramatic returns for apartment owners and developers.

Nevin explains which states are likely to prosper most and why the US is demographically safer than the rest of the industrialized world. Read this book, smile, and make wiser choices. You'll probably be wealthier, more confident, and better informed."

—**Terry Moore, MBA,** author of *Building Legacy Wealth*

"A cross between John Naisbitt's *Megatrends* and Isabel Wilkerson's *The Warmth of Other Sons*, Nevin has shown us how today's world is shifting, evolving, and reshaping itself. Data rich, with entertaining narrative, the author does not hold back or equivocate in putting forth predictions in *The Next Half Century.* Whether you agree with his conclusions or not, this is an essential read for the thoughtful person who wants to understand where we are headed and what to expect."

—**Cheryl Soon,** Ph.D., Fellow, American Institute of Certified Planners and author of *Reflections in Stone and Bronze*

THE
Next Half
Century

Prepare for an
Amazing Change
in World
Prosperity

THE
Next Half
Century

ALAN NEVIN

This book contains the opinions and ideas of its author. It is intended to provide helpful and informative material on the subjects addressed in the book. Although the author and publisher have made every effort to ensure that the information in this book was correct at press time, no liability is assumed for losses or damages due to the information provided.

Published by Global Economic Press

To contact the author about speaking or ordering books in bulk, visit www.nevinadvisors.com

ISBN (paperback): 979-8-9886144-0-1
ISBN (deluxe color paperback): 979-8-9886144-1-8
ISBN (ebook): 979-8-9886144-2-5

Editor: David Aretha
Book design: Christy Day, Constellation Book Services
Publishing consultant: Martha Bullen, Bullen Publishing Services
Indexer: Amy Murphy
Author photo: Steve Johnson, GAFCON

Library of Congress Control Number: 2023913400

Printed in the United States of America

Contents

Introduction

The Next Half Century is a book about the world tomorrow. It is a compelling story of the future that you and your heirs will experience.

This is a book about trends, past and future, based on research drawn from demography and, to some degree, real estate. I am both a demographer and a real estate economist, so I blend the two practices in order to project the future.

Demography is the study of people: how they live, how they grow, and how they fit within the societies they live in. **If you know demography, you will know the future of the world.**

The book does have a lot of numbers, but in the words of statistician W. Edwards Deming, "without data you're just another person with an opinion."

I am not an academician and therefore this is not a textbook. It is a rather readable story about the future of the **United States** and its growth patterns (with an emphasis on the states that are at the heart of the economy). This book also discusses four population centers that are large enough to make a difference in the world tomorrow: **China, India, Russia,** and the **European Union/United Kingdom.**

It is these five entities that account for a majority of the world's production of goods, including oil, merchandise, and brainpower. They are the powers that the United States must deal with on a daily basis if it is to remain in a dominant position as the world's No. 1 power.

Pessimism blankets the world today, much of it relating to the Russian invasion of Ukraine. Some of it relates to China's threats to Taiwan and North Korea's playing with nuclear weapons.

I don't want to belittle that triad of misery, but we have to look beyond that to envision a world that is on the cusp of massive improvements in economics, education, and lifestyle.

It's remarkable to consider that in the 1990s only 1.0% of the global population had access to the World Wide Web. Today, two-thirds of the world can see what life is like in First World countries. Internet access whets the appetites of people who live in developing countries to crave education and a better way of life. In the past three years, more than one billion people have gained access to the Web.

A major part of the next half century will witness the economic growth of developing countries—countries that will experience a substantial decline in fertility coupled with a major increase in education, employment, and incomes.

Many of these countries will become Second World countries and be in the same league as China and India. They will produce the goods that are required to satisfy the needs of an expanding world.

Economically speaking, we will see a dramatic increase in world gross domestic product, a meaningful reduction in fertility rates, a lessening of starvation, improving literacy, and the uplifting of the lifestyles of billions of people.

Much has been written about the potential failure to feed the masses in developing countries. It is my contention that the severe reduction in fertility will mean that there will be a food supply/demand balance in the decades ahead.

Equally positive, First World countries will provide the tools, education, and financing to lift developing countries out of the misery they suffer today.

And, finally, the United States will be at the forefront of the massive economic changes that lie before us.

Snapshot of the 12 Chapters

Chapter 1: As the World Turns

Chapter 1 takes a well-rounded view of the economy of the world and its output, both in terms of business and people.

This chapter blends the world of business with demography, melding the growth patterns of economies with the changing patterns of households and childbirth. The chapter is a prelude to Chapter 2.

Chapter 2: Demographics: An Aging World

This chapter delves into the aging patterns in the world, focusing on this century's demographics.

Demography determines the future of the world, more than interest rates, politics, or climate. As we look into the balance of this century, we see one overarching trend: a reduction in the number of births per female. And that reduction is as prevalent in First World as it is in developing countries.

The reduction in births in developing countries will allow them to prosper and be healthier, more educated, and safer, and will also promote gender equality.

And, as the prime theme of this book, the United States will take the lead on the betterment of these countries, and, in the process, provide them with the consumer goods, healthcare, and lifestyle that we take for granted.

Following the theme of demography is the continual movement of the world's population. It is a movement that will not cease and will inevitably find its way to other democratic countries, or, better yet, cause non-democratic countries to change their ways.

Chapter 3: Rusting Russia: A Failed Nation Facing Bad Times

A country with never-ending problems. Russia never recovered from the 25 million citizens (mostly male) who were killed during World War II. In recent decades, they have also faced a major exodus of educated people and are woefully lacking in technological advances.

As a result of these deaths, the number of household formations following the war was meager and, concomitantly, the birthrate dramatically declined. Even today, three-quarters of a century after the conclusion of World War II, the birthrates in Russia are dismally low. This situation has been exacerbated by the "the brain drain" and the accelerating rate of Russian citizens leaving the country as a result of the Ukrainian war.

The multiple socio-economic problems of Russia are discussed in depth in this chapter, including alcoholism, corruption, crime, suicide, a failing education system, and a dismal economy.

Chapter 4: A Changing China: One from Column A and One from Column B

China is an amazing country, having created a powerful economic machine in less than a quarter century and the ability to support more than a billion people. Its brand of politics isn't admirable, but it has learned how to provide food and jobs for the multitude of its population. Unfortunately, its population is shrinking and there is little they can do about it.

Chapter 5: India: The World's Largest Democracy

It is the largest democracy in the world, four times larger than the U.S., but maintains Second World status. It has the will and the brainpower to move forward in world status and is only now taking major strides to improve its education system and to reduce its fertility rate.

Chapter 6: The European Union and Great Britain: Modestly Growing Economic Powerhouses

The twenty-eight countries that comprise the European Union are an amazingly strong congregation of highly educated and capitalistic First World countries that act as one. The United Kingdom is included in this chapter even though it is no longer in the EU. Combined, they are the second largest economic machine in the world (the U.S. is No. 1).

Chapter 7: California: The Land of the Free, Home of the Ingenious

California is the fifth largest nation in the world in terms of GDP. It has developed a remarkable university system and superb nonprofit scientific organizations, and has proven to have magnetic powers to attract great minds and great money.

With a population of 40 million and almost 10% of the U.S. Congress, California is a powerhouse that is slowly being chipped away at by Texas and a few other Southwest states.

Having said that, California has a remarkable array of good jobs in a myriad of industries and clearly dominates the world of pharmaceuticals and social media and to a lesser extent, software.

And, as mentioned, California has an enviable bank of universities including the entire U.C. system, Stanford, USC, and a multitude of high-quality smaller colleges like the Claremont Colleges, University of San Diego, and Cal Tech.

Chapter 8: Texas: A State Worth Bragging About

Texas deserves a chapter of its own because it is a major source of good jobs, reasonably priced homes, and a huge draw of people from California, especially those who lean to the right.

Oil is the financial underpinning of the state and that allows the state to have a myriad of fine colleges and hospitals and to keep its streets paved and public safety at the forefront—something that California has not yet mastered.

Chapter 9: South Atlantic States: The South Is Rising Again

The South Atlantic states in this book include Florida, Georgia, and North and South Carolina, all hugging the Atlantic Ocean.

Florida does not have great universities or great nonprofit institutions, but it does have warmer weather than the states north of the Mason-Dixon line. It also has relatively inexpensive housing, taxes, and consumer goods. It will continue to drain the North.

Georgia and North and South Carolina are job machines and an intricate part in the "drain the North" program. And Georgia and North Carolina have a cadre of very good universities that draw the upper tier of millennials to their core.

Chapter 10: Moving Up Through Sharing: Prepare for an Amazing Change in World Prosperity

As the United States shares its wealth and its brainpower with the rest of the world, in the next half century, we will see incredible improvements in the lives of those who now suffer from the ills of decayed societies and warped economies. Stay tuned to a far better tomorrow.

Chapter 11: Climate Change in the United States: It's Not Going Away

Here is a realistic look at climate change in the United States, focusing on the states that will feel the brunt of the changes and the human and financial costs associated with them.

Chapter 12: Why the U.S. Will Remain the World's Economic Driver

The U.S. will remain No. 1 because it welcomes brainpower from all over the world and encourages emigration from nations that have not created a science-friendly environment. Every nation has its coterie of fine minds—it's just that in many, or most, nations, they don't take advantage of those minds. And those great minds move on.

The discoveries of tomorrow will create prosperity throughout the world, and the U.S. will provide most of those discoveries. The inventiveness of the United States has allowed it to dominate the world of science and technology. But it hasn't done it alone; the U.S. has fostered the in-migration of great minds and endless venture capital.

Education is the key to enduring economic prosperity. The U.S. STEM education system is producing an enviable number of engineers, scientists, healthcare professionals, and software and hardware entrepreneurs who are exploding the world of ideas.

The weak spot is that not everybody in the U.S. is given the opportunity to participate in the STEM world. That will change.

The United States is as varied in prosperity and economics as are the other countries of the world. The concentration of venture capital in a half dozen metropolitan areas is astounding and continuous. It is those same half dozen metropolitan areas that have the nation's foremost universities and nonprofit scientific institutions. The smartest of the smart gravitate to those meccas, leaving the balance to hobble along. A few new "brain centers" will materialize as well.

CHAPTER 1

As the World Turns

As the industrialized countries grow, so do our opportunities for doing business abroad, with the west coast of our nation in a particularly strong position to benefit from international growth if for no other reason than its proximity to the South American countries and the countries in the Far East.

In this section, I will cover the growth of the gross domestic product, household incomes around the world, and the **opportunities for sharing our knowledge** with countries on the move.

As a preface, it is notable that in 1850 64.0% of the American population earned its living through farming. By 1900 that figure had fallen to 38.0% and today, in 2023, it is 2.0%.

From an international perspective, those living on less than $2.00 a day (the World Bank's threshold for "extreme poverty") has declined by more than half in the past thirty years from nearly two billion to 700 million. This decline relates to declining fertility and improving economies.

Gross Domestic Product (GDP) of the World

Gross domestic product is the sum of all goods and services produced in a country. **The world GDP was negligible until the 1700s when**

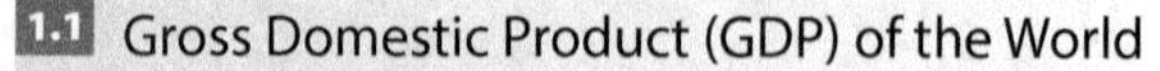

1.1 Gross Domestic Product (GDP) of the World

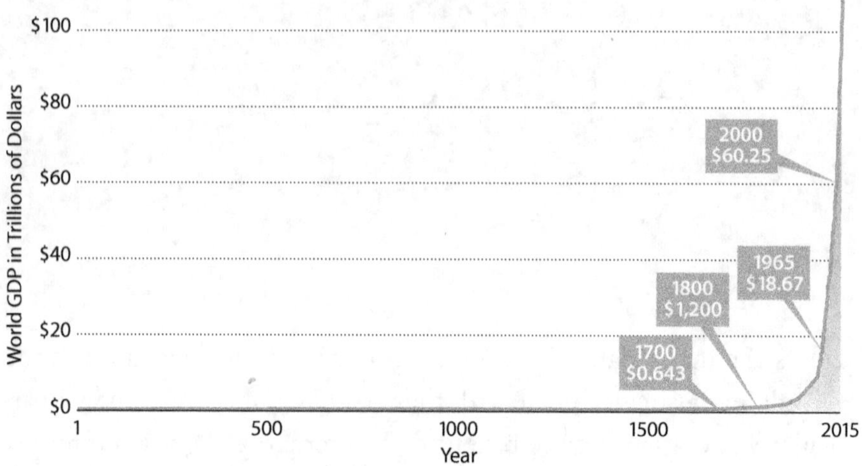

Source: World GDP – Our World in Data based on World Bank and Maddison (2017)

industrial tools were created.

The GDP of the world is **approaching $100 trillion** and is likely to hit that mark by 2025. That will be the kick-off point for projecting the balance of the 21st century.

Virtually every major country in the world had a negative gross domestic product in 2020, thanks to COVID. With COVID mostly under control in the First World countries, the GDPs in near-term future years are projected to be positive.

1.2 World GDP (Trillions) 2016–2022[1]

Year	Trillions	Index
2016	$76,439	1.00
2017	$81,359	1.06
2018	$86,347	1.13
2019	$87,607	1.15
2020	$84,705	1.11
2021[F]	$89,702	1.17
2022[F]	$94,097	1.23

1. Forecast

Source: World Bank

**1.3 Economic Outlook
Gross Domestic Product
Major Countries, 2020–2022**

Country	2020	2021	2022
World Output	**–3.2%**	**6.0%**	**4.9%**
U.S.	**–3.5%**	**7.0%**	**4.9%**
Germany	–4.8%	3.6%	4.1%
France	–8.0%	5.8%	4.2%
Japan	–4.7%	2.8%	3.0%
China	2.3%	8.1%	5.7%
India	–7.3%	9.5%	8.5%

Source: International Monetary Fund

On a **per capita basis**, there have been some remarkable increases in the past two decades. **The GDP for the world more than doubled.** The major increases have been in **India** and **China**, up 351% and 1,140% respectively.

**1.4 Gross Domestic Product Per Capita
Selected Countries, 2000–2021**

Country	2000	2010	2020	2021	Change 2000–2021 Dollars	Change 2000–2021 Percent
World Output	**$5,487**	**$9,555**	**$10,925**	**$12,290**	**$6,803**	**124%**
U.S.	**$36,334**	**$48,466**	**$63,543**	**$69,375**	**$27,209**	**75%**
China	**$959**	**$4,550**	**$10,500**	**$11,891**	**$10,932**	**1140%**
India	$443	$1,357	$1,900	$2,000	$1,557	351%
Germany	$23,695	$41,572	$46,215	$50,788	$27,093	114%
Canada	$24,271	$47,462	$43,258	$51,987	$27,716	114%
France	$22,364	$40,638	$40,298	$45,028	$22,664	101%
Japan	$38,532	$440,507	$40,113	$40,704	$2,172	6%

Source: International Monetary Fund

Despite the major increases in China and India, the **U.S. has a per capita GDP six times that of China and 35 times that of India.** Admittedly, India and China started with a much lower base, but it is still very impressive.

Median Household Income (Per Capita)

It is no surprise that the nation with the highest median household income per capita (of those shown in Exhibit 1.4) is the United States, but it is important to note that our neighbor to the north, Canada, is fast approaching the household income of the United States.

As Canada is a major importer of our goods, it is very positive that their household incomes are about the same as those in the United States.

1.5 Median Household Income Per Capita, Major Countries, 2021

Country	2021
United States	**$19,306**
Canada	**$18,652**
Germany	$16,845
United Kingdom	$14,793
Japan	$14,543
South Korea	$12,507
Russia	$5,504
China	$4,246
Mexico	**$3,315**
India	$1,314

Source: World Bank, United Nation

Our neighbor to the south, Mexico, does not provide the United States with a meaningful market for the goods we produce as their median household income is about 15% that of the U.S.

INTERNATIONAL MIGRATION—A HALLMARK OF FREEDOM

Though rarely a topic of discussion, international immigration has been enormous in recent years. In the past 40 years, the number of migrants worldwide has tripled. Today, **almost 250 million people live and work outside their country of birth,** and 90% of them do so voluntarily to improve their economic prospects. The other 10% are refugees and asylum seekers due to unstable or hostile environments.

THE MAJOR PLAYERS AND THEIR ROLE IN THE WORLD

As we look at the world in coming decades, there are six countries that will continue to be **dominant players** in the world economy: the U.S., China, India, Russia, the United Kingdom, and Germany. Each has its individual strengths and weaknesses.

There are several others that have decent economies and produce nice goods, but they are not major political players on the world scene. For instance, Japan, South Korea, and France.

First, let us look at the future of these countries in terms of population:

**1.6 Projected Population Growth
Selected Major Countries, 2020–2050**

Country	2020	2050	Total	Percent
Russia	145,934,000	135,824,000	(10,110,000)	–6.9%
Germany	83,784,000	80,104,000	(3,680,000)	–4.4%
China	1,439,324,000	1,402,405,000	(36,919,000)	–2.6%
United Kingdom	67,886,000	74,082,000	6,196,000	9.1%
United States	331,003,000	379,419,000	48,416,000	14.6%
India	1,380,004,000	1,639,176,000	259,172,000	18.8%

Source: United Nations Department of Economic & Social Affairs, Population Division

Germany is a manufacturing powerhouse, but it has an exceptionally low birthrate and does not look favorably on immigration. Therefore, it is projected to have a declining population base over the next few decades.

China is only now beginning to recover from its one-child policy, but it had 30 years of that policy and the future generations are getting smaller. In addition, very few people want to immigrate to China. Its birthrate has plummeted for each of the past six years.

Russia is also a country that is declining in growth. It's a combination of low birthrate and very minor net in migration.

Great Britain, the **United States**, and **India** will continue to grow, even though their birthrates are declining. Two later chapters expound on these two countries.

In demographic terms, in First World countries, **it is necessary to have two children per two adults** in order to form a more perfect union. In other words, if you want your country to grow (and prosper) a couple (married or not) has to have two kids.

Of the six key countries, only India is achieving the 2.0 ratio, but also notice the major decline in the birthrate in India and China.

1.7 Birth Rates[1]
Six Major Countries, 2022

Country	1970	2022
India	5.6	2.2
United States	2.5	1.7
China	5.7	1.7
Great Britain	2.4	1.6
Germany	2.2	1.5
Russia	2.0	1.5

1. Births per 1,000 women aged 15–44

Source: United Nations

In the following exhibit, pay particular attention to the change in the percent of the population in these five countries for persons **under age 18**. Focus on China and Japan.

1.8 Comparison of Major Countries
Population & Fertility Factors

Factor	United States	India	China	Russia	Japan
Population					
2020	331,003,000	1,380,004,000	1,439,324,000	145,934,000	126,476,000
2050	379,419,000	1,639,176,000	1,402,405,000	135,824,000	105,804,000
Change	48,416,000	259,172,000	(36,919,000)	(10,110,000)	(20,672,000)
% Change	15%	19%	–3%	–7%	–16%
Percent of Population Under Age 18					
1980	28%	45%	43%	26%	28%
2020	22%	32%	21%	21%	15%
Fertility					
1980	1.80	4.85	2.52	2.04	1.70
2020	1.78	2.24	1.69	1.82	1.37

Source: World Bank, International Monetary Fund

If you don't have two kids, then your country better have a strong immigration program. Unfortunately, **India, China,** and **Russia** have a very weak immigration attraction. The U.S. continues to be the most attractive to newcomers.

1.9 Immigration by Country
Six Major Nations, 2021

Country	Total Population	Net Migration	Immigration as Percent of Population
India	1,380,004,000	(2,663,000)	–0.193%
China	1,439,324,000	(1,742,000)	–0.121%
United States	331,003,000	477,000	0.144%
Great Britain	67,215,000	270,000	0.402%
Germany	83,240,000	208,000	0.250%
Russia	145,934,000	106,000	0.073%

Source: Moody's Analytics; World Bank

Let's look at the big six from the standpoint of **Exports** and **Imports**:

Exports

The exhibit below notes the output of goods for the major countries. The U.S. is obviously not a big player in the export business. The U.S. appetite for goods is so strong that it can absorb almost everything it produces.

Countries that heavily rely on exports for their existence cannot afford to anger the countries that buy their goods.

Conversely, the same countries whose economies rely on exports have a heavy reliance on imports. And, as notable, the U.S. does not import much.

1.10 Exports as % of GDP
Major Nations, 2020

Nation	% of GDP
United States	8.5%
Japan	15.5%
China	18.5%
India	18.7%
Russia	25.5% i s
Great Britain	27.9%
Korea	36.4%
Germany	43.4%

Source: World Bank

Imports

Now let's look at the big eight in terms of their gross domestic product, imports, and exports:

The United States

The United States' GDP is almost equivalent to that of the other five countries in total. As the rest of this book is heavily devoted to the United States, I will not dwell on it here, except to say that the U.S. continues to be the world leader in virtually every economic category and is responsible for providing economic security for the rest of the world.

When we look at the past 50 years in the world, we see that the United States' GDP was lightyears ahead of the rest of the world and the

1.11 Imports as Percent of GDP Major Nations, 2020

Nation	% of GDP
United States	**13.3%**
Japan	15.5%
China	16.0%
India	19.2%
Russia	20.6%
Great Britain	27.7%
Korea	32.8%
Germany	37.7%

Source: World Bank

1.12 Gross Domestic Product (Trillions of Dollars) Major Countries A 50-Year Picture, 1970–2020 World

Country	1970	Percent of World	2020	Percent of World
World	**$12.14**		**$87.70**	
United States	$1.07	**8.84%**	$21.43	**24.44%**
China	$0.09	**0.76%**	$14.34	**16.35%**
Japan	$0.21	1.70%	$5.08	5.79%
Germany	$0.20	1.67%	$3.86	4.40%
India	$0.06	0.51%	$2.87	3.27%
United Kingdom	$0.12	1.01%	$2.83	3.23%
Russia	$0.21	1.70%	$1.70	1.94%
South Korea	$0.08	0.66%	$1.65	1.88%
Mexico	$0.04	0.32%	$1.27	1.45%

Sources: World Bank, Directorate of Intelligence, CIA

world is just now catching up. The U.S. accounts for almost one-quarter of the world GDP.

"The world catching up" is a highly positive trend as expansion of a country's gross domestic product is a positive event.

Russia

Russia is a rapidly declining country. Fifty percent of its government's revenue comes from oil. It does very well when oil is expensive and essentially goes bankrupt when it declines substantially. That's not a particularly good formula for economic survival. Russia's only strong manufacturing industry is weapons of war that they can sell to Mideast sultans. When was the last time you went into an auto showroom to test drive a Russian SUV?

Their best minds have steadily emigrated to the United Kingdom, Israel, and the U.S.

Russia supplies virtually all of Europe's vehicles with gasoline products. What happens when the EU goes all electric? (And it will.) As it is, European cars get 50 MPG.

The Ukrainian war drags on and there appears to be no end in sight. It is difficult to obtain accurate numbers, but it does appear that more than 100,000 Russian soldiers have been killed or wounded. The Russian Armed Forces currently have 1.15 million active-duty personnel.

And, as an added economic wound, more than 5 million Russians have moved out of Russia since the beginning of the war. Emigrants have moved to 38 countries according to the UN Commissioner for Refugees. More than 50,000 Russian information technology specialists have left Russia.

China

China is a problem child. It has enormous potential but is hampered by a static, actually declining population.

Its exports equal 18.5% of its GDP compared to 8.5% of the United States' GDP. China, therefore, has to be a huge export machine in order to remain solvent. To do that, they have to play nice. If Walmart cuts off purchases from China for two weeks, China could go bankrupt (a small exaggeration). The reality is that China must continue to produce goods that will appeal to every country because they can't consume everything they produce.

China plays the bad guy and tries to beat up Taiwan and other Far East countries, but they can't do too many nasty things or the countries they sell to will invoke stringent sanctions and ruin them.

Plus, Xi Jinping likes Americans. He speaks very good English and his daughter graduated from Harvard.

P.S.: Goods produced in China are no longer bargains and they are farming out their manufacturing to other developing countries. More on that later.

India

India is the world's largest democracy. That won't get them much if they can't figure out how to feed all their people and move to Second World status. I know they have the brainpower and the energy, but they desperately need to curtail their birthrate and to power up their manufacturing and technical output.

Only 8.0% of the Indian adult population has a college degree. The U.S. total is 36%. The other Indian problem is that it only has a literacy rate of 74%. It's segmented into 82% of males and 65% of females.

P.S.: Seventy-two percent of adults immigrating to the U.S. from India have a college degree.

Germany

Germany is a manufacturing powerhouse, certainly the most proficient and profitable in the European Union. No other country even comes close. It has been under wonderful leadership for a couple of decades and that really helped keep the country on top. It just keeps rolling along. Its education system, including vocational studies, is excellent.

The only things hurting them are that they don't have a vibrant source of young labor that can work its way up into better jobs and they don't have a great tolerance for immigrants.

In addition, they sell more than 19 billion dollars in vehicles to China, so they must remain friends with them.

Great Britain

Brexit has not been a brilliant success, as the majority of Brits are beginning to realize. Nonetheless, it is a major financial capital and has an exceptionally bright and educated population. Not quite bright enough to defeat Brexit, however (the vote was 52% to 48%).

The media have not been kind to Great Britain since Brexit, and the press regularly takes potshots at the politics that continue to plague the country. Brexit has had a negative effect on exports (something that the Brits must have in order to survive). Most pointedly, Great Britain has severe supply line problems.

It is a melting pot. The "native" population of Great Britain mirrors that of the United States in terms of a low birthrate. The good news is that Great Britain has a large Middle Eastern population that tends to have many children. Over the past two decades, the fastest-growing type of household in Great Britain was that with multiple generations and many children. Since 2000, there has been an increase of 275,000 multiple-family households with an average of seven people.

OPPORTUNITIES ABOUND FOR THE U.S. IN THE DECADES AHEAD

For the past few decades, the U.S. has allowed China and a few other countries to be the major suppliers of manufactured goods to the U.S. I believe that situation will change over the next few decades.

Washington has finally realized that by acquiring goods from China, Russia and other countries that are not particularly friendly to the U.S. is giving away the store.

It is my contention that the U.S. will gradually revitalize its manufacturing base both by executive fiat and by tax-friendly programs for manufacturers.

No doubt the automobile industry will take the lead in returning to on-shore manufacturing. Along with that will come a return of the major parts that relate to the automobile industry including steel, plastics, batteries, tires, and the myriad of items that fall into the category of replacement parts.

1.13 U.S. Manufacturing Output, 2000–2020

Year	Billions of Dollars	Index	Percentage of GDP
2000	$1,549	1.00	15%
2010	$1,791	1.16	12%
2020	$2,337	1.51	11%

Source: FRED

The U.S. manufacturing output has been dependably increasing in the past decade, but not as a percent of GDP. In other words, the economy is growing faster than its manufacturing output. And that's not necessarily a bad thing.

1.14 Employment
Top Five Manufacturing Industries
United States, 2020

Industry	Number of Jobs
Food Manufacturing	1,516,396
Fabricated Metal Products	1,343,492
Machinery	1,019,740
Transportation	1,527,970
Plastics & Rubber Products	770,616

Cumulative Change in Percent of Manufacturing Employment from 2005–2022

Source: U.S. Census Annural Survey of Manufacturer

This exhibit shows the top five U.S. manufacturing industries and the jobs they create:

The following exhibits demonstrate the growth of manufacturing employment in the U.S. from 2005-2021:

1.15 Change in Manufacturing Employment United States, 2005–2022

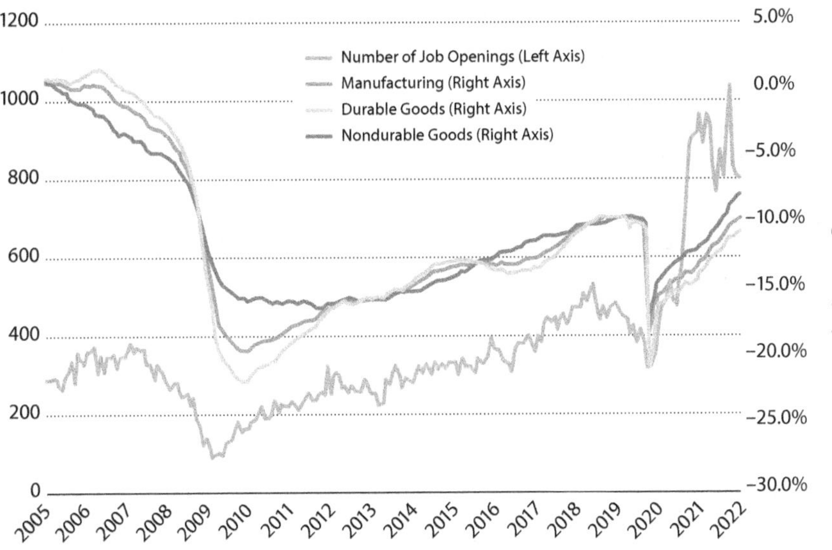

Source: Bureau of Labor Statistics

The World Economic Forum ranks 141 countries on **competitiveness**. The following exhibit notes eight of the components of their index. The U.S. ranks highly in the index.

Based on its ranking of 152 countries, the U.S. is among the top five in terms of competitive industrial performance.

1.16 World Economic Forum Competitiveness Index Indicators U.S. Ranking out of 141 Countries

Component	Rank
Airport Connectivity	1
Companies embracing disputive ideas	2
Ease of finding skilled labor	1
Electrication rate	2
Mean years of schooling	7
Quality of research institutions	1
Road connectivity index	1
Scientific publications	1

Source: World Economic Forum

The Kearny "reshoring index" looks at the U.S. percentage of its goods that are imported from China. Until COVID, it was clearly on a downhill path and is now back to where it was pre-COVID. Kearny anticipates that it will begin again its path to reducing China's share of U.S. goods.

1.17 Rankings from the Competitive Industrial Performance Index (152 countries), 2020

Country	Rank
Germany	1
China	2
South Korea	3
United States	4
Japan	5

Source: UN Industrial Development Organization

1.18 United States Percentage of Imports from China[1]
1Q2013–4Q2021

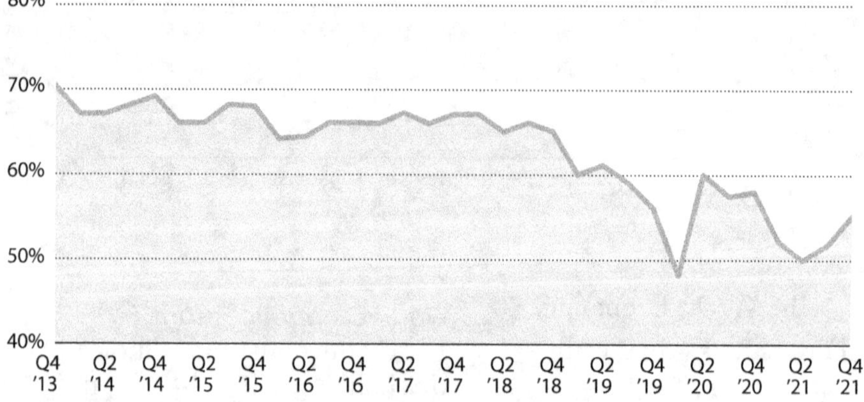

1. Includes U.S. imports from Hong Kong. LCC is low-cost country.

Sources: Kearney Global Management; United States International Trade Commission

Reshoring

Bringing manufacturing back from abroad (known as reshoring) is back on the front burner. Last year, Congress passed the CHIPS Act, which provides $52 billion in funding to revive semiconductor manufacturing in the U.S. plus billions more for research and development.

This reshoring is mandatory because Taiwan hosts the world's most advanced semiconductor manufacturing facilities, producing 90% of the world's most powerful chips. And their proximity to China is not favorable, to say the least.

Reportedly, the U.S. brought back 350,000 jobs from overseas in 2022.

Climate Control: Global Warming

The U.S. should be taking the lead on limiting global warming. Action is necessary to limit global warming to roughly 1.5 degree Celsius by the end of the century.

Acquiring Materials and Components

Currently, China has 76% of the world's lithium battery production capacity and 60% of the rare-earth metals needed for building electric vehicles, wind turbines, and solar energy. The U.S. needs to change that situation.

GLOBAL DEMAND

"As in the past, there is an immediate and powerful global demand for cheap and reliable products. In the mid-19th century, it was foodstuffs and in the 1970s, it was oil and commodities. In the 2020s, it is medical supplies, data chips, and rare earth metals. To be resilient, these commodities need to be produced and traded internationally, by a multiplicity of suppliers."

—Professor Harold James, Princeton University

Now, on to Chapter 2.

CHAPTER 2
Demographics:
An Aging World

Chapter 1 dwelled heavily on the world of business and education. In Chapter 2, I turn to the subject of aging—a very important part of the economies of the world. The subject of aging relates to (1) the size of the labor force, (2) the future strength of the consumer market, and (3) the cost associated with the health and welfare of the aged.

For most industrialized countries, at least a quarter of their population is over age 60, with the U.S. not far behind.

2.1 Population by Age
The Oldest Major Countries as of 2022

Country	Percentage 60+	Percentage 70+	Percentage 80+
Japan	34%	22%	9%
Italy	30%	18%	8%
Germany	29%	16%	7%
France	27%	15%	6%
UK	24%	14%	5%
United States	**23%**	**11%**	**4%**
Russia	22%	10%	4%
South Korea	23%	11%	4%

Source: United Nations Population Section

SECTION 1: AGING IN THE UNITED STATES

The United States offers a good example of the aging pattern. According to the Census Bureau, in the 2020-2060 timeframe, folks 65 and older will increase almost 70%.

2.2 Population by Age Group, United States, 2020–2060

Age Group	2020	2040	2060	Percent Change 2020–2060
	In Millions			
Under 18	74	77	80	8.1%
18–44	119	126	133	11.8%
45–64	83	89	97	16.9%
65 and older	**56**	**81**	**95**	**69.6%**
Total Population	332	373	405	22.0%

Source: U.S. Census Bureau

2.3 Projected Adult Population, Age 65+, United States, 2016–2060

By 2060, nearly one in four Americans is projected to be an older adult.

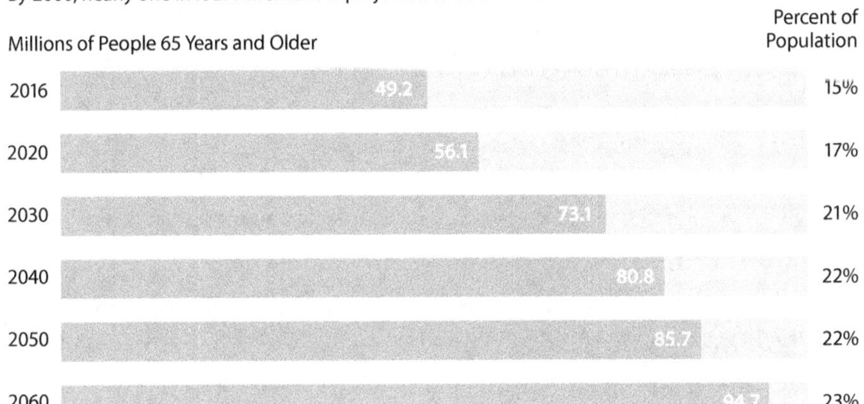

Sources: 2017 National Population Projections; U.S. Census Bureau

The long-term implications of an aging population are economically troubling and discouraging. But more on that later.

"Overall, 2021 will go down as the year with the slowest population growth in U.S. history."

—Miriam Jordon and Robert Gebelof, *New York Times*

The sluggish growth is due to three elements: the number of births has fallen sharply in recent years, the number of deaths has increased (partially COVID-driven), and the gain from immigration has declined.

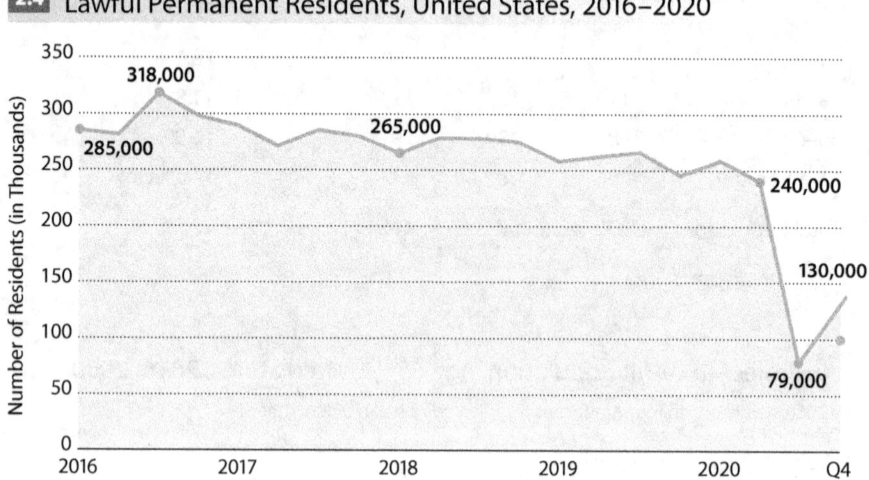

Note: Fiscal years end on September 30 of years shown. Figures are rounded to nearest 1.000.

Source: Pew Research Center (Based on U.S. Department of Homeland Security)

"In 2008, persons aged 16-17 were growing at a rate of 200,000 a month. Right now, that population is growing at 25,000 a month. The biggest change is in 20-30 year olds. Up until five years ago, that population was growing by 50,000 a month. Now it's declining by 50,000 a month."

—James E. Glassman, Managing Director, JP Morgan Chase & Co.

It appears that with lower birthrates and higher death rates, the only way the U.S. can grow is through immigration. In 2021, new residents from other countries totaled a quarter million. This is still substantially lower than in previous decades when the U.S. often had 1.0+ million immigrants. But the Trump administration put the brakes on immigration and it gradually ebbed downward until the Biden administration.

Currently, immigrants represent 13% of the U.S. population, compared to 12% one hundred years ago. **Notably, the U.S. has more immigrants than any other country in the world.**

2.5 Native and Foreign Born Population United States, 1920–2020

Year	Percent Foreign Born	Native-Born	Foreign Born	Total
1920	13.2%	105,710,020	13,920,692	119,630,712
2020	15.5%	285,400,000	44,100,000	329,500,000
1920		88%	12%	100%
2020		87%	13%	100%

Source: 1920 and 2020 Census

The Census Bureau has projected foreign-born population out to 2060. By 2060, the percent of foreign-born is expected to be 17.1%.

2.6 Foreign-Born People Living in the United States
1850–Projected to 2060

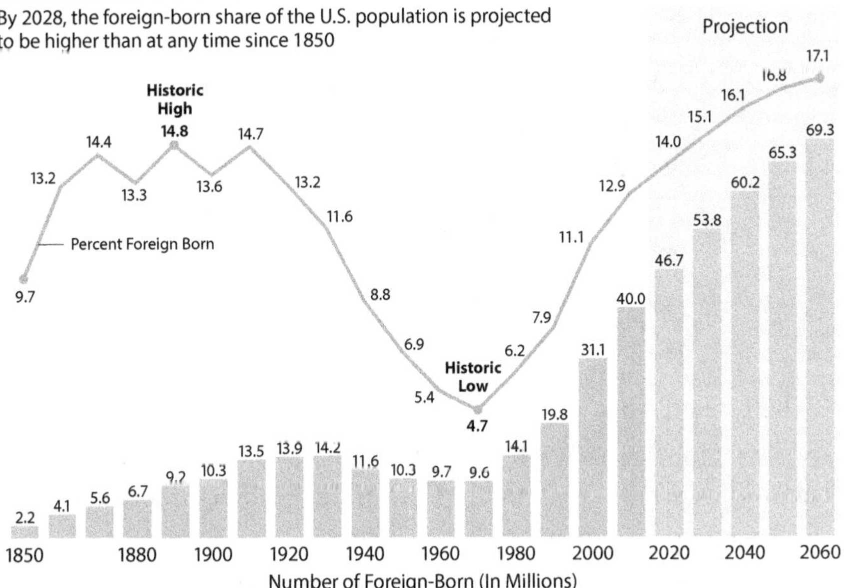

Sources: Census 1850–2000; American Community Survey 2010; 2017 National Population Projections for 2020–2060

Looking back through history, in the 1920 census, the percentage of foreign-born persons was 13.2%, almost the same as today.

2.7 Place of Birth and Ethnicity, United States, 1920 Census

Ethnicity	Total	Percentage	Foreign Total	Percent Foreign
White	94,820,915	89.70%	13,712,754	14.5%
Negro	10,463,131	9.90%	73,803	0.7%
Indian	244,437	0.23%	6,299	2.6%
Chinese	61,039	0.06%	43,107	70.6%
Japanese	111,010	0.11%	81,338	73.3%
All Other	9,488	0.01%	3,391	35.7%
Total	105,710,020	100.00%	13,920,692	13.2%

Source: 1920 Census

This chart shows the origin of immigrants to the U.S. in 2020:

2.8 Origin of U.S. Immigration Population, 2020

Europe and Other North America	13%
Asia	28%
Other Latin America	25%
Mexico	25%
Africa and Other	9%
Total	100%

Source: Pew Research Center

The foreign-born population is increasingly concentrated among **middle-age groups**. About one in five Americans between the ages of 40 and 64 were born overseas. And two-thirds of foreign-born residents have been in the country more than a decade.

Within the U.S., the **foreign-born homeowners** tend to be concentrated in coastal areas. In this exhibit, we show the top 10 metropolitan areas with the highest share of foreign-born homeowners. **Notably, five of the top 10 are in California**.

2.9 Metropolitan Areas with Highest Share of Foreign-Born Homeowners

Rank	Metropolitan Area	Percentage	Rank	Percent Foreign	Percentage
1	San Jose	45.0%	6	Riverside	28.0%
2	Miami	43.9%	7	Houston	26.8%
3	Los Angeles	37.3%	8	Las Vegas	25.4%
4	San Francisco	33.3%	9	San Diego	24.1%
5	New York	28.9%	10	Washington D.C.	22.8%

Source: Lending Tree; Census American Community Survey

SECTION 2: FOLLOW THE FERTILITY

In the exhibit below, I show that countries like Japan and China are losing population at a rate that does not augur well for their economies. Japan is, by far, the biggest loser among the world's mature nations. **In the next 40 years, Japan will lose almost one-quarter of its population** and it's almost too late to do much about it.

The three major Asian countries (Japan, China, and South Korea) have negligible in-migration so cannot depend on that source of new population, unlike the U.S.

2.10 Population (In Millions), Major Countries, 2020–2060 (Projected)

Country	2020	2060	2020–2060 Change	Percent Change
United States	325,700	404,500	78,800	24%
Viet Nam	103,808	121,833	18,025	17%
South Korea	51,245	46,900	(4,345)	–8%
Russia	142,021	126,898	(15,123)	–11%
European Union	448,825	432,470	(16,355)	–4%
Japan	127,141	99,100	(28,041)	–22%
China	1,410,539	1,286,294	(124,245)	–9%

Source: United Nations Population Division

In 2021, there were more than one-half million applications for asylum in the EU. Four countries accounted for two-thirds of the applications: France, Spain, Italy, and Germany.

2.11 Asylum Applicants European Union, 2021

Country	Number of Applicants	Percent
Total	537,355	100%
Germany	148,175	28%
France	103,790	19%
Spain	62,050	12%
Italy	45,200	8%
Total	359,215	66%
Other 24 Countries	178,140	34%

Source: European Union Eurostat

Despite the fact that a majority of the asylum seekers are young, the median age in the EU is creeping up with one out of five over age 65.

2.12 Age of Population European Union, 2012–2022

Year	2012	2022
0–14	15%	15%
15–64	67%	64%
65+	18%	21%
Total	100%	100%
Median	41.0	44.4

Source: Eurostat

The exhibit below tells a very vivid story about the future of the **European Union** of 28 countries. In about 20 years, given their present rate of fertility and in-migration, they will begin to decline in population.

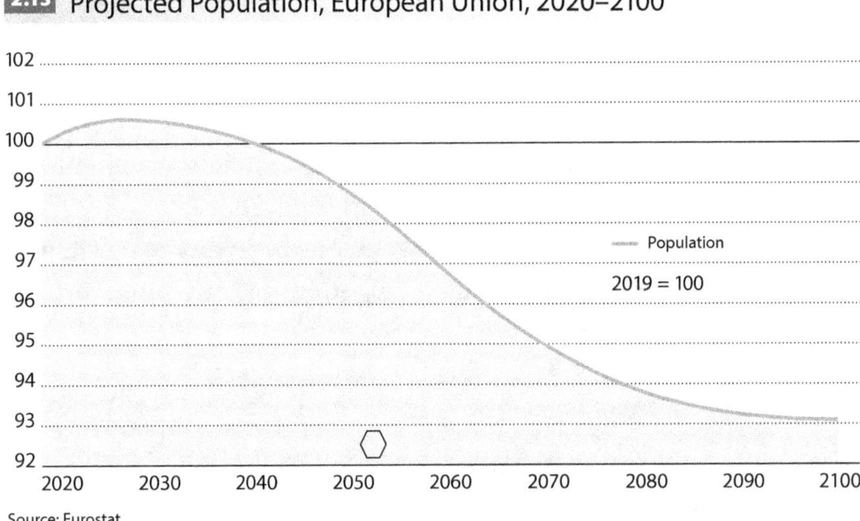

Source: Eurostat

The implications of this aging pattern are not pretty as the working-age population declines on a very dependable basis and the demands of Social Security, social services, and healthcare expand, as shown on this Eurostat graph:

China Population Problem

In pure numbers terms, China is the big loser. Starting with the one-child rule of the Mao generation, the fertility rate in China plummeted. This year, China announced that its birthrate declined for a fifth straight year.

The falling Chinese birthrate, coupled with the increased life expectancy, means that the number of persons of working age, relative to the growing number of people too old to work, has continued to decline.

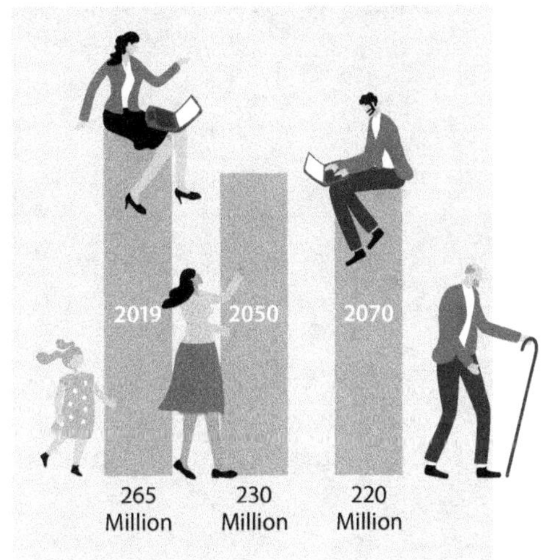

2.14 Working Age Population, European Union, 2019 Projected to 2070

Source: Eurostat

Pointedly, that could result in major labor shortages that, in turn, could hamper economic growth and reduce the tax revenue needed to support an aging society.

China's ruling Communist Party now allows as many as three children. It is also offering incentives to young families and promising improvements in workplace rules and early education.

In China, the current number of persons born this past year was equal to the number who died. Not a good sign for China.

SECTION 3: THE FERTILITY RATE

The fertility rate (children per woman) in the industrialized countries is on a steady decline.

2.15 Fertility (Children Per Woman)
Major Countries, 1990–2060 (Projected)

Country	1990	2020	2040	2060
India	3.81	2.10	1.80	1.74
France	1.80	2.03	1.78	1.71
United States	**3.03**	**1.84**	**1.83**	**1.83**
Mexico	3.33	1.67	1.75	1.71
United Kingdom	1.72	1.62	1.67	1.70
Russia	1.87	1.60	1.60	1.60
China	2.21	1.45	1.56	1.60
Japan	1.49	1.38	1.52	1.66
Germany	1.23	1.36	1.65	1.70
Spain	1.16	1.27	1.56	1.70
Italy	1.18	1.22	1.52	1.68
South Korea	1.69	1.10	1.29	1.40

Source: United Nations

The long-term decline in most of the countries can be chalked up to several factors:

- Women are entering the workforce and remaining in it for much longer than in the past, thereby delaying childbirth, often as late as age 40.

- The number of persons reaching retirement age has caused employers to offer benefits for employees to stay on the job longer, a situation that has been particularly attractive to women who ordinarily would have had children earlier in life.

- The cost of living in most of the countries has increased substantially in recent years, resulting in women working longer in order to live better and bolster their savings.

Japanese demographers project that a woman born in Japan in 1990 has close to a 40% chance of having no children of her own and a 50% chance of never having grandchildren.

The key to economic solvency in the First World countries is to have **2.0 children per household**. France is the only First World country that meets that standard, with the U.S. not far behind. Most of the other First World countries are far behind in that category.

The French fertility rate meets the 2.0 level because of two factors: a substantial number of foreign-born women and, of more importance, France has generous pro-child policies and childcare is well organized (i.e., there is gender equality).

Japan is a primary example of how to economically survive when your fertility rate is low and your senior population is growing rapidly. They have looked to other countries to produce their goods, particularly cars. For instance, Toyota has 125 plants around the world. Therefore, the profits from those cars allow Japan to be economically solvent and to support the growing number of retirees with health and welfare services.

The U.S., on the other hand, currently has sufficient labor in all age groups to produce everything it needs or wants.

SECTION 4: EVOLVING COUNTRIES

The major population gains in the next 40 years will be in the populous **Evolving Countries,** as noted below. Note, however, that the fertility rates have subsided dramatically in most of these populous countries as they strive to achieve more capitalistic economies.

2.16 Fertility (Children Per Woman)[1]
Evolving Countries, 1990–2060 (Projected)

Country	1990	2020	2040	2060 as Percentage of 2020
Iran	5.32	1.94	1.70	32%
Afghanistan	8.00	4.82	2.60	33%
Iraq	6.00	3.10	2.14	36%
Pakistan	5.80	3.60	2.22	38%
Viet Nam	3.53	2.05	1.70	48%
Nigeria	6.03	4.72	3.03	50%
Egypt	3.45	3.11	1.99	58%
Brazil	2.78	2.38	1.71	62%

1. Women age 15–45

Source: United Nations

Despite the projected reduction in children per woman, these countries will experience substantial population growth over the next 40 years, as shown here:

2.17 Population Projections
Evolving Countries, 2020–2060 (Projected)

Country	2020	2060	Change	Percent Change
Afghanistan	38,346,000	71,937,000	33,591,000	88%
Nigeria	213,986,000	515,386,000	301,400,000	141%
Iraq	38,828,000	69,817,000	30,989,000	80%
Pakistan	233,431,000	403,522,000	170,091,000	73%
Iran	84,038,000	101,418,000	17,380,000	21%
Viet Nam	101,745,000	121,833,000	20,088,000	20%
Egypt	103,994,000	162,616,000	58,622,000	56%
Brazil	214,752,000	234,439,000	19,687,000	9%
India	1,389,000,000	1,646,862,000	257,862,000	19%
Total	**2,418,120,000**	**3,327,830,000**	**909,710,000**	**38%**

Source: census.gov/data-tools/demo/idb/#/country

If you are keeping score, you will observe that the mature countries (like the U.S. and the others in Exhibit 2.10) will be losing 91 million population **by 2060 while the evolving countries (Exhibit 2.18) will add almost a billion population.**

In total, between now and 2060, the world population will expand by 2.5 billion persons, or an annual rate of 65 million. The median age will grow, but very slowly.

2.18 Population Change
Major Mature and Evolving Countries, 2020–2060

Year	In Thousands	
	Mature	Evolving
2020	2,609,279	2,418,120
2060	2,517,995	3,327,830
Change	(91,284)	909,710
Percent Change	–3.5%	37.6%

Source: Census Bureau Population Division

Thus, the world will grow steadily in the next 40 years. In a future chapter, I will delve into how these evolving countries are moving forward toward Second and occasionally First World status, but it's a long road.

2.19 Projected Future World Population, 2020–2060

Year	Population	Median Age
2020	7,800,000,000	29.7
2060	10,381,000,000	31.6
Change	2,581,000,000	
Annual Change	64,525,000	

Source: United Nations Dept of Economic and Social Affairs

SECTION 5: CONCLUSION FOR THE UNITED STATES

Looking to the future, retirees and soon-to-be retirees in the First World countries have to figure out how to prepare for longer lives.

In this decade, **more than 24.0 million Americans will reach age 65 by 2030:**

2.20 Aging Population, Persons Over Age 65
United States, 2020–2030

Year	Persons 65+		
	Men	Women	Total
2020	25,014	31,037	56,051
2030	40,216	40,216	80,432
Change	15,202	9,179	24,381

Source: Census Bureau Population Division

And with an aging population come the costs of expanding healthcare. The healthcare costs in the United States continue to increase. **From 1980 to 2020, expenditures have increased by a factor of 10.**

2.21 Life Expectancy and Health Care Expenditures
United States, 1980–2020

Year	Life Expectancy	Health Care Expenditure Per Person	Inflation Adjusted[1]
1980	73.7	$1,036	$1,036
2020	78.9	$11,945	$1,260

1. average inflation 1980–2020 3.04% per annum

Source: Peterson KFF Health Care Tracker 2021 (Peterson Center on Healthcare)

The U.S. healthcare expenditures are substantially higher than in other First World countries (and their life expectancies are the same as in the U.S. or higher). In the other countries, healthcare is socialized.

2.22 Annual Health Care Costs
Selected First World Countries, 2021

Country	Expenditures	Life Expectancy
United States	**$11,945**	**77.3**
Japan	$4,691	84.6
France	$5,564	82.2
Canada	$5,370	81.8
Netherlands	$6,299	81.4
Germany	$6,731	80.9
United Kingdom	$5,268	80.9

Source: KFF Health System Tracker

Financially challenged, the healthcare costs of the U.S. must be reduced. It appears that the most logical ways for that to happen are to :

- Continue reducing the time patients remain in a hospital after surgery or procedures;

- Continue the major expansion of clinics in drugstores utilizing the services of nurse practicioners, rather than MDs;

- Substantially expand "traveling medical services" and somehow

- figure out how to substantially reduce the administrative costs associated with health care (now approaching 25%).

The costs of building and maintaining hospitals is untenable. It is not just the bricks and mortar. It's the costs relating to physically maintaining the premises, the utility bills, and the FFE (fixtures, furniture, and equipment).

In California, the older hospitals do not meet current seismic standards and must be replaced. The cost of replacement is obnoxiously expensive.

Why not set a national goal of reducing healthcare expenditures to match those of Europe?

The U.S. is the only advanced economy that does not offer universal healthcare coverage. In 1948, Harry S. Truman made a major effort to introduce national health insurance, but obviously was not successful.

ARE SENIORS DESTINED TO LIVE OUT THEIR LIVES IN POVERTY?

An endless stream of articles and books has been published in recent years that lead to a conclusion that seniors will live out their lives in poverty or maybe just surviving on Social Security.

Nothing could be further from the truth.

More than 26 million seniors own a home and two-thirds of them are debt-free.

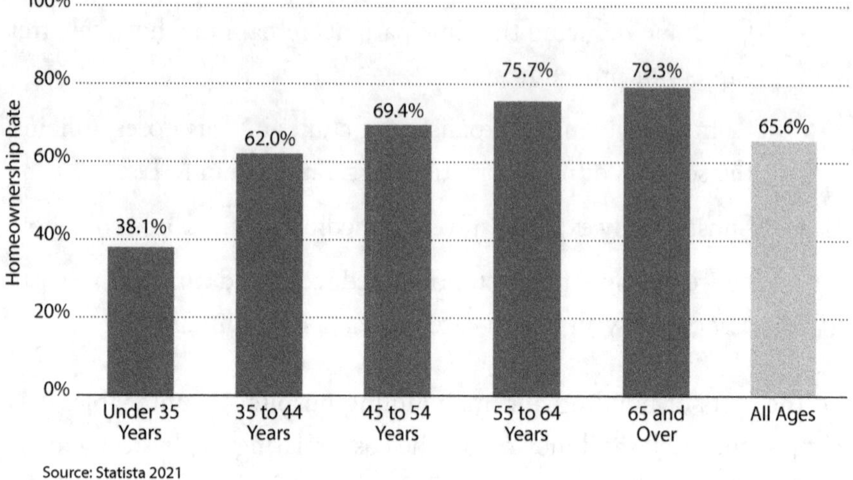

2.23 Home Ownership Rate by Age of Homeowner United States, as of First Quarter 2021

Source: Statista 2021

The average home price (U.S. 2022) is $348,000, and more in some places:

The equity totals more than **five trillion dollars**. Reverse mortgages are a viable option.

A second major source of benefits is **life insurance**. In 2021, life insurance companies paid out benefits of more than $100 billion. As most of that is whole life, it can be a major source of borrowing for seniors who are cash short.

And we must not forget Social Security, which has recently increased its benefits and is a tidy sum each month, even after the Medicare deduction.

2.24 Average Home Price Selected States, 2022

State	Value
California	$763,358
Florida	$366,301
Texas	$285,664
New York	$250,003
United States	$348,079

Source: CAR, NAR

2.25 Estimated Assets Persons 65+, United States

Source	Amount
Life Insurance Benefits Paid Out 2021	**$100,188,000,000**
Home Ownership	79%
Homes Owned by Persons Over 65	26,311,000
Percent Owned Debt-Free	62%
Homes Owned Free and Clear	16,312,820
Average Home Price (U.S. 2022)	$348,079
Total Equity	**$5,678,150,072,780**

Source: American Council of Life Insurers; and American Housing Survey

Payments to beneficiaries continue to rise, and typically one-half of the couple passes away before the other half so the surviving spouse has a decent source of capital.

2.26 Payments Life Insurance Beneficiaries United States, 1980–2021

Year	Millions of Dollars	Index
1980	$12,884	
1990	$24,567	1.91
2000	$44,143	3.43
2010	$58,392	4.53
2021	$100,188	7.78

Source: American Council of Life Insurers

Four states account for one-third of the payments to beneficiaries:

2.27 Payments to Life Insurance Beneficiaries, 2021

State	Thousands	Percentage
California	$13,238,654	9%
Florida	$9,465,509	7%
Texas	$11,069,505	8%
New York	$9,249,425	6%
Big 4	**$43,023,093**	**30%**
Other 46 States	$100,773,830	70%
Total	$143,796,923	100%

Source: American Council of Life Insurers

A new study from UCLA Professor Lee Ohanian shows in the U.S. the senior population has had a major increase in income in the past 30+ years. In the exhibit below, it shows the source of income in the 1982 to 2018 timeframe.

2.28 Sources of Income Among All Seniors (2020 Dollars) United States, 1982–2018

Year	Mean Income	Retirement	Labor Earnings	Investment	Social Security
1982	$43,400	$4,700	$10,400	$14,100	$13,400
2018	$91,900	$20,400	$22,700	$23,700	$22,300
Percent Change[1] 1982–2018	112%	332%	119%	67%	66%

1. Inflation adjusted

Source: Lee Ohanian, Professor of Economics, UCLA

Overall, most seniors are in rather decent shape financially (just ask the cruise ship companies).

2.29 Real Growth in Median Income (Inflation Adjusted) United States, 1982–2018

Marital Status	Seniors	Non-Seniors
Married	108%	49%
Single Female	81%	21%
Single Male	68%	5%
Age		
Under 65		23%
65–69	43%	
70–74	108%	
75 and Older	146%	
Education	47%	5%
Some College	27%	1%
Bachelors degree or higher	58%	20%

Source: Lee Ohanian, Professor of Economics, UCLA

SECTION 6: HOUSING SENIORS

Given the forthcoming explosion of seniors in the U.S., providing housing specifically for that aging group is imperative.

The types of housing can be segmented into three: **subsidized, market-rate and assisted living.**

Subsidized Units

There are numerous firms throughout the nation that have been providing subsidized senior housing for seniors. According to PAHRC (Public & Affordable Housing Research Corporation), there are almost 3.0 million seniors living in subsidized housing in the U.S. They have also tabulated a current need for another 3.6 million units for seniors who have less than 80% of median housing income and pay more than 30% of their incomes for rent.

Market Rate Housing Units

Market rate units for seniors with more than 100% of median housing income comprise the largest percentage of seniors. Typically, seniors with more than 100% of median housing income own their homes and, in most cases, have no mortgage. The home-owning sector accounts for 70% of seniors. Notably, the over-55 sector has the highest net worth of any age group because of the equity in their homes

The problem is that home-owning seniors are most often living in homes that are of a size relating to when they had children living with them and, if an opportunity presented itself, they would move to smaller quarters, most often in senior communities.

The major problem in the United States is that there are remarkably few communities that are designed for seniors. It is a market that remains largely untapped, with the exception of a few states like Florida and Arizona.

Certainly, Florida and Arizona are attractive from a climate standpoint, but most seniors want to remain near their children and friends and medical and other services that are a major part of their lives.

As noted in the beginning of this report, in the next 40 years, there will be 39 million Americans 65 years of age or older. Their appropriate housing accommodations for seniors are paramount if we are to free up housing for younger households.

Assisted Living

This category is most often the least affordable and most expensive housing for seniors. This category can be segmented into two predominant categories: (1) housing for able body folks who are content living in a hotel-like environment and (2) housing for those who are disabled and need continual nursing care. In the first category, the housing may be either "buy-in or traditional rentals.

SECTION 7: BOLSTERING IMMIGRATION: THE KEY TO A THRIVING TOMORROW IN THE U.S.

The key to a thriving future in the U.S. is fostering immigration of tomorrow's workforce. We currently allow immigration of 1,000,000 annually and have achieved that in each of the past 30 years.

But the U.S. really needs to foster immigration of 1,500,000+ in order to grow and prosper.

Canada has the same aging problem that the U.S. has and has taken aggressive steps to welcome appropriate newcomers to their nation.

Canada welcomes immigrants under three classes: economic class, family class, and refugee and humanitarian class.

The Economic Class: Canada needs skilled workers to support its labor force and economic growth.

The Family Class arrives through family sponsorship. Allowing close family members to build a life in Canada provides families with the opportunities to thrive in a new country.

Refugees and Humanitarian Purposes: Canada has claimed a moral obligation to provide safety to those fleeing persecution and other hardship.

Canada aims to welcome well over 400,000 immigrants every year (into a nation with fewer people than live in California). Two-thirds of these immigrants arrive as skilled workers and can immigrate through the Express Entry management system.

SECTION 8: TWO CLOSING THOUGHTS ON AGING

Thought 1:

Despite the strong asset base, senior Americans and those in other First World countries will most probably have to **work longer** and **save more** to prepare for a longer life. There just aren't enough younger Americans to fill the labor void. In Japan, 25% of the workforce is over age 65.

In 2007, Germany increased its retirement age from 65 to 67 and most other European countries have since followed suit. Some have started indexing their retirement ages to rising life expectancy. And the French are rioting against a proposed increase in retirement age.

The U.S. isn't far behind.

Thought 2:

A not so small problem that the U.S. is facing: Americans are dying younger on average than they used to, younger, for instance, than in China. This bizarre fact is explained not by middle-aged or elderly but by the deaths of young people. One in 25 American 5-year-olds won't live until age 40, a death rate about four times as in other wealthy nations.

Firearms account for almost half of the increase in deaths. Car crashes and accidental drug overdoses account for 18.4%, according to the *Journal of American Medicine*. Suicides account for fewer than 10%.

Black men, on average, can expect to live five fewer years than white American men, a lower life expectancy than in Rwanda or North Korea.

Almost two-thirds of the victims of homicide in the U.S. were non-Hispanic Blacks ages 10 to 19, a rate six times as high as that of Hispanic children and 20 times higher than white children.

Per David Wallace-Wells in the *New York Times*, "America is a violent place and getting more violent."

CHAPTER 3

Rusting Russia: A Failed Nation Facing Bad Times

"Russia: It is fitting that Russia is at the bottom of the list on everything. It is a nation that has nothing going for it but oil. Large segments of its educated population have moved out; the birthrate is plummeting, the median age is rising, and the government only cares about enriching itself. "Things have been going wrong in Russia since Catherine the Great. And she died in 1797."

—Russian General

In this treatise, I explore the long-standing problems with the Russian economy, including its demographic, social, health, and financial challenges.

SECTION 1: TERMINAL DEMOGRAPHY: AN AGING NATION

The study of the future of any nation inevitably begins with a study of its demography and two principle elements: the **ratio of children-bearing-age women to men** and, concomitantly, **the natural birthrate**.

A basic demographic premise: For a **First World economy** to grow and prosper, it is necessary to have two children for every man and woman. That can occur through the traditional process of a couple having children or through in-migration. The key to continual prosperity is continued population growth. Both are key to a continual prosperity predicated on increasing population growth.

On June 22, 1941, Hitler's Wehrmacht invaded the Soviet Union to initiate what would become the most brutal and costly war between two countries in history.

The surprise attack on the woefully unprepared Red Army led to devasting losses for the Soviet Union in the early phase of the war. Within the first six months, the Red Army had lost **nearly 5 million men**—the size of the Soviet Union's entire prewar army.

Only a portion of that loss was recovered in the decade after the war. It has been on a slide since 1990 (World Bank Russian annual population growth).

3.1 Population Russia, 1930–2020

Year	Population	Change
1930	100,948,000	
1940	110,333,000	9,385,000
1950	102,798,657	(7,534,343)
1960	119,871,700	17,073,043
1970	130,148,653	10,276,953
1980	138,053,150	7,904,497
1990	147,531,561	9,478,411
2000	146,404,903	(1,126,658)
2010	143,479,274	(2,925,629)
2020	145,934,452	2,455,178

Source: Macrotrends

The past few years provide some indication of the future of Russia:

3.2 Annual Population Change Russia, 2015–2020

Year	Population	Change	Percent Change
2015	144,985,057	n/a	
2016	145,275,383	290,326	0.2%
2017	145,530,082	254,699	0.2%
2018	145,734,038	203,956	0.1%
2019	145,872,256	138,218	0.1%
2020	145,934,462	62,206	0.0%

Source: Macrotrends

Emigration/Immigration

Russia suffered major population losses in the 2000-2010 period. Vladimir Putin came into office in 2000. Five million people left Russia during the first 20 years of his rule.

A recent study revealed that one in five Russians wanted to emigrate, with younger people twice as likely to want to emigrate than older Russians. The study found that 55% of those who actually left Russia were between the ages of 20 and 40. Of those, 92% had a university degree and 14% had a Ph.D.

Net migration (the difference between the number of persons entering and leaving a country during the year) in Russia is 1.7 migrants per 1,000 population compared to 3.8 for the United States.

Each year, fewer and fewer people immigrate to Russia:

3.3 Net Migration Russia 2005–2020

2005–2010	2,327,000.00
2010–2015	1,801,000.00
2015–2020	912,000.00

Source: United Nations

Russia's Birthrate

By the end of World War II, Russia suffered 25 million military and civilian casualties, resulting in an imbalance in population between men and women.

Even by the 21st century Russia still had the **lowest overall male-to-female ratio in the world**, especially among the elderly.

The irregularities of this ratio will continue to have an impact on the number of births and the rate of population growth and aging for several decades. Russia has more deaths each year than births:

Based on research by the U.S. Census Bureau and the United Nations, Russia's population will shrink from 146 to 111 million by 2050, a loss of 35 million people.

3.4 Men to Women Russia 2005–2020

Year	Men	Women
1950	76.6	100.00
2020	86.8	100.00

Source: United Nations

3.5 Births and Deaths Russia 2020

Births	1,435,750
Deaths	2,124,479
Net	(688,729)

Source: United Nations

3.6 Projected Change in Population through 2100, Russia

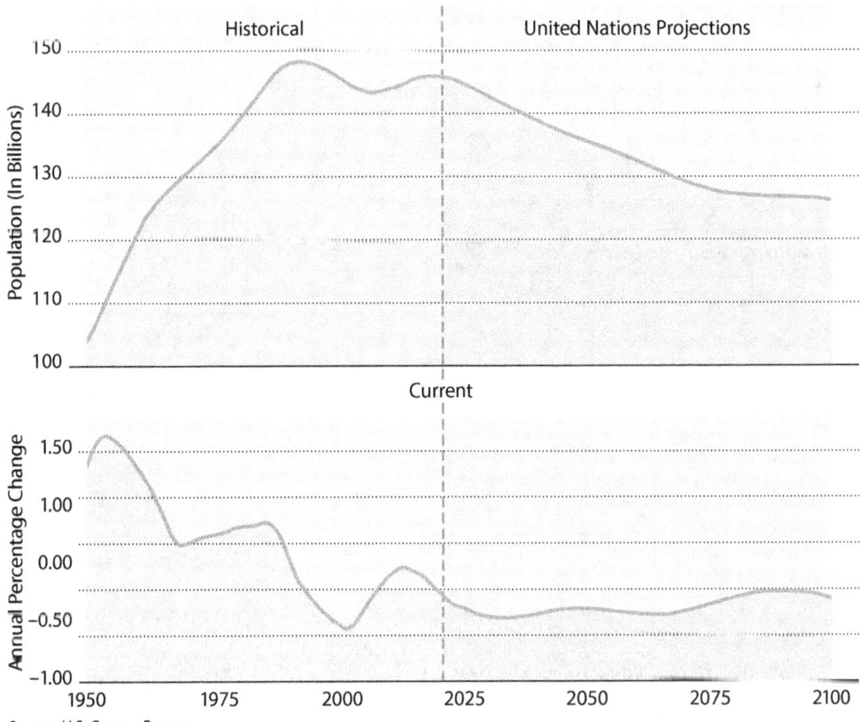

Source: U.S. Census Bureau

There are multiple factors involved in this decline:

1. Fertility Rate

The Russian fertility rate of births per women ages 15-45 has been steadily sinking since 1970 with a 50-year low in 2000.

In 2006, Putin directed his nation's parliament to develop a plan to reduce the country's falling birthrate. The president called on parliament to provide incentives for couples to have a second child in order to stop the country's plummeting population. Those incentives had a short-term positive effect.

3.7 Total Fertility Rate Russia 1970–2020	
Year	Fertility Rate
1970	2.02
1980	1.88
1990	1.90
2000	1.55
2010	1.98
2020	1.74

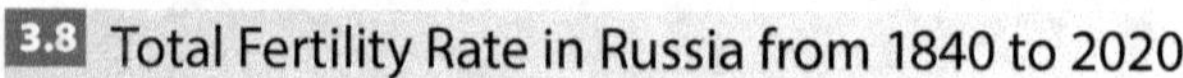

3.8 Total Fertility Rate in Russia from 1840 to 2020

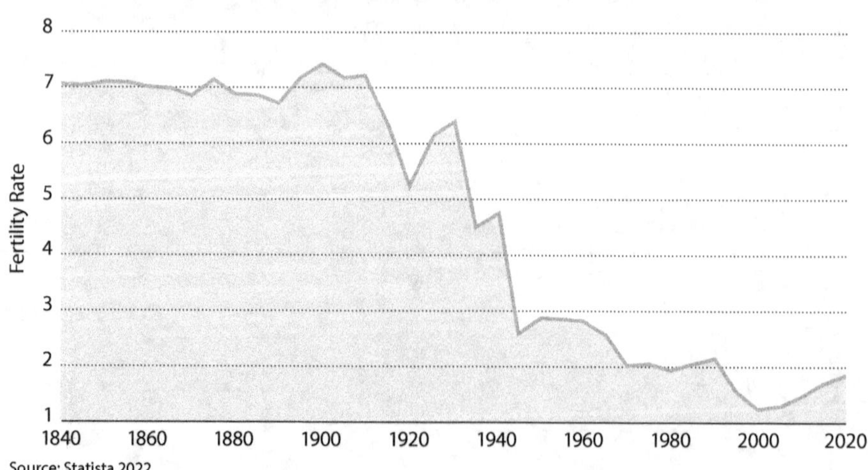

Source: Statista 2022

Russia, unfortunately, also has other problems that coincide with the fertility rate:

2. Abortions

Many Russian women use abortion as their sole course of birth control. According to a 2017 article in *Foreign Policy Magazine*, Russia has a ratio of around 480 abortions per 1,000 live births, compared to 200 per 1,000 in Europe and the U.S.

3. High Death Rate

Russia's death rate is 13.4 per 1,000 people each year. This compares with 8.2 per 1,000 in the United States and 9.4 in the United Kingdom. The death rates relate to poor healthcare, alcoholism, and smoking.

The life expectancy of Russian males is significantly lower than many other nations—including countries with much lower economic bases:

Projections for the balance of this century indicate that Russia's life expectancy will pale in comparison with other First World countries.

3.9 Life Expectancy, Males Russia and Other Countries

Country	Life Expectancy (years)
Israel	81.0
Japan	81.0
U.S.	76.3
China	75.0
Egypt	70.0
Russia	**68.2**
India	68.0

Source: World Bank

3.10 Future Life Expectancy Major Countries, 2020–2099

Country	2020	2099	Change	Percent Change
United States	79	89	10	13%
Germany	81	91	10	12%
China	77	88	11	14%
Russia	**72**	**84**	**12**	**17%**
Japan	85	94	9	11%

Source: United Nations

4. Alcoholism

Alcoholism is rampant in Russia. A recent survey of 60,000 men revealed that four out of five drink at least a half-liter of vodka each week. The other one-fifth of the men drank more.

3.11 Vodka Consumption by Men, Russia

Consumption	Respondents	Percentage
1/2 litre per week	63,964	81%
1–3 half litre bottles	12,050	15%
More than 3 bottles per week	2,842	4%
Total	78,856	100%

Source: World Health Organization

5. Smoking

Concomitant with alcohol consumption is smoking. The vodka consumers typically smoke a pack a day.

3.12 Smoking Characteristics
Vodka Consumption by Men, Russia

Consumption	Respondents	Current Smoker	Cigarettes Per Day
1/2 litre per week	63,964	69%	16.10
1–3 half litre bottles	12,050	86%	19.10
More than 3 bottles per week	2,842	89%	21.30
Total	78,856		

This graph shows the death rate for Russian men compared to those in the United Kingdom:

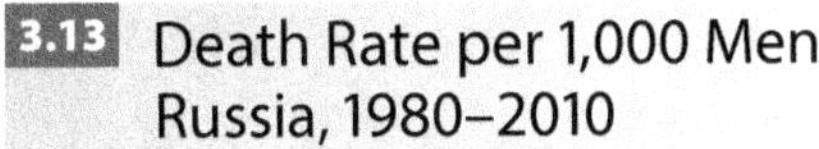

3.13 Death Rate per 1,000 Men Russia, 1980–2010

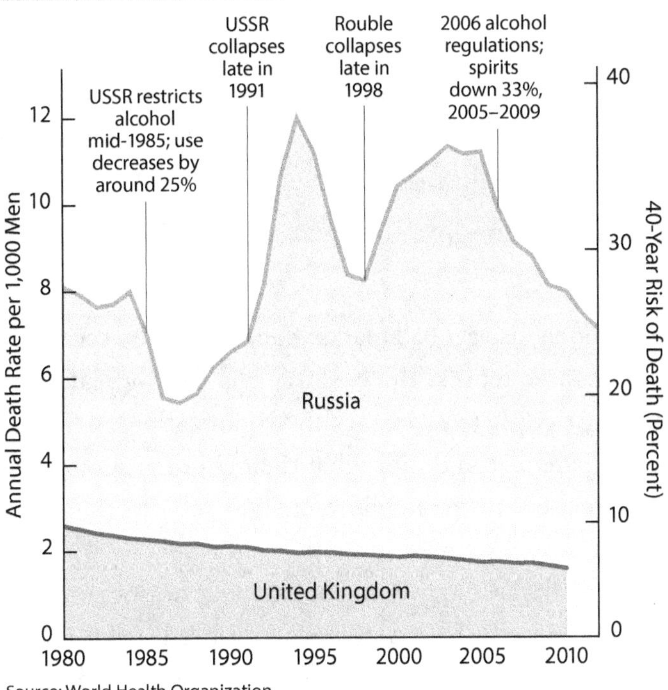

Source: World Health Organization

6. Ravages of Disease

"Tuberculosis (TB) is highly endemic in Russia. It is a major public health problem in this country and there is a rising incidence of multi-drug-resistant TB."

—International Association of Medical Assistance of Travelers (IAMAT)

Bacterial "superbugs" are getting ever more potent. Tuberculosis strains in Russia carry mutations that not only make them resistant to antibiotics but also help them to spread more effectively. This is according to an analysis of 1,000 genomes from different TB isolates—one of the largest whole-genome studies of a single bacterial species so far.

SECTION 2: EDUCATION SYSTEM

"Russia has implemented reforms aimed at giving pupils an equal shot at a good education. But the introduction of centralized university entrance exams has so far failed to end corruption in the school system."

—Evlalia Samedova, Deutsche Welle (DW) Russian Service

Russia's schools also get bad marks when it comes to social concerns—with serious consequences. **The country has the highest suicide rate among young people** (World Health Organization).

In Russia, parents can decide what their children should learn. Very often, the parents want their children taught subjects that the teachers may not be educated to provide.

Apparently, Mr. Putin's government has made drastic cuts to financing for education. Today in Russia, there is a vast redistribution of money from education, health, science, and culture in favor of the huge military, police, and state administration spending. **In the 2012-2016 period, federal spending on education decreased 26%.**

In the 2008 to 2018 period, the percent of the gross domestic product that was expended on education declined from 4.10% to 3.20%.

3.14 Government Spending
Education as Percent of GDP
Russia, 2000–2018

Year	Percent of GDP
2000	2.90%
2008	4.10%
2018	3.20%

Source: United Nations

The per capita expenditures on education have declined in the past decades.

SECTION 3: THE RUSSIAN ECONOMY

Russia's GDP, on a per capita basis, ranks among the lowest in First World countries and only marginally above China and Brazil. Its per capita GDP is one-sixth that of the United States.

The annualized GDP for the past decade is shown in this graph. Note the severe decline in GDP in 2015 and 2016. That decline was the result of the Russian invasion of Crimea and a precipitous fall in oil prices. In 2014, the price of oil per barrel fell from $100 in May to $60 in December. Reportedly, Russia needs to have $100 per barrel to achieve a balanced budget.

3.15 Gross Domestic Product Per Capita Major Countries, 2022

Country	GDP	GDP/Capita
United States	$20.50	$59,939
Canada	$1.71	$44,841
Germany	$4.00	$44,680
France	$2.80	$39,827
United Kingdom	$2.80	$39,532
Japan	$4.97	$38,214
Italy	$2.00	$32,038
Russia	**$1.50**	**$10,846**
Brazil	$1.87	$9,881
China	$13.40	$8,612
India	$2.70	$1,980

Source: Worldometer

3.16 Annualized Gross Domestic Product, Russia, 2012–2022

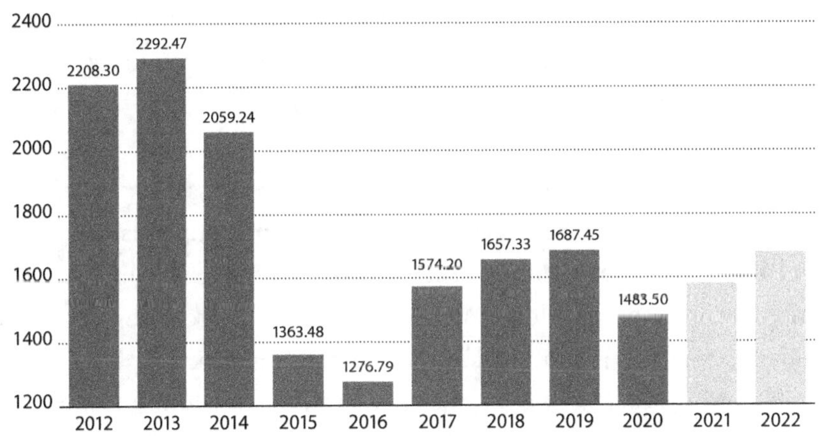

Sources: Trading Economics; World Bank

Note the decline in 2020 on the above graph from effects due to the COVID pandemic, which interrupted a rising GDP just as Russia was on a path to economic recovery.

Russia manufactures very little. Eight of its top 10 exports are natural resource based:

3.17 Russian Global Shipments, 2021

Product	Billions of Dollars	Percentage	Natural Resource	Percent Natural Resource
Mineral Fuels including oil	$211.5	62.5%	X	62.5%
Gems, Precious Metals	$31.6	9.3%	X	9.3%
Iron, Steel	$28.9	8.5%	X	8.5%
Fertilizers	$12.5	3.7%	X	3.7%
Wood	$11.7	3.5%	X	3.5%
Machinery including Computers	$10.7	3.2%		
Cereals	$9.1	2.7%	X	2.7%
Aluminum	$8.8	2.6%	X	2.6%
Ores, Slag, Ash	$7.4	2.2%	X	2.2%
Plastics, Plastic Articles	$6.2	1.8%		
Total	**$338.4**	**100.0%**		**95.0%**

Source: Fintech 250

Before the Ukraine war, 30-35% of the Russian government's revenues were **oil sales**. In 2023, oil revenues have fallen to 20-25% of the budget (U.S. Treasury Department). Researchers attributed three-quarters of the fall to lower sales volume and larger price discounts for Russian crude—both factors directly related to Western restrictions (*Financial Times*, April 26, 2023).

As a result of the diminution of revenue, the Russian population is suffering as they depend heavily on governmental stipends.

Russia does have the benefit of **mining minerals** that are very important to the development of chips. Russia produces neon and palladium, which are important in chip manufacturing.

According to *Fortune* magazine, Ukraine is a leading exporter of **highly purified neon gas**, which is necessary for the lasers that are used

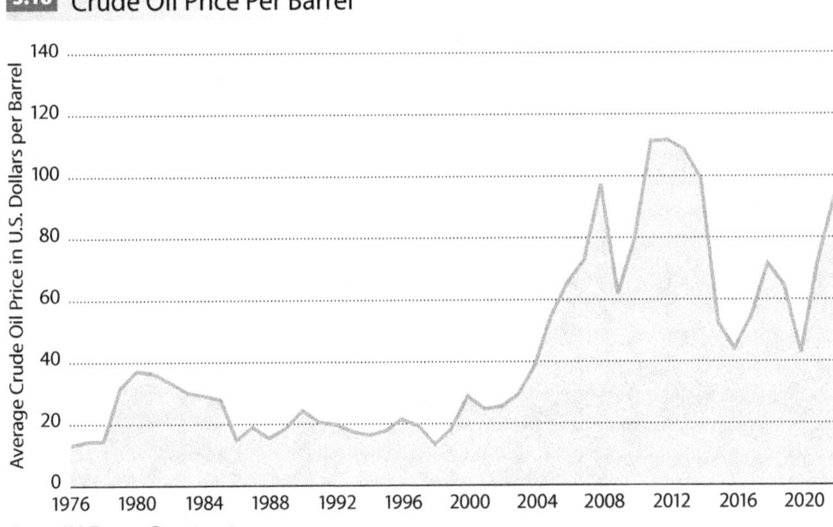

Source: U.S. Treasury Department

to etch circuit designs into silicon wafers to create chips. And disrupting their economy will cause a shortage of the neon. The last time Russia invaded Ukraine, in 2014, the price of neon shot up 600%.

Russia is the world's leading producer of **palladium**, which is essential for many memory and sensor chips. The country also produces several other key raw materials for computer chips, including the rare-earth scandium.

Russia and Ukraine together account for almost one-third of world **wheat production** with much of that shipped to countries in the Middle East and North Africa. The price of wheat has risen to some of the highest levels seen in a decade. The Russians import Chinese labor to assist with the harvesting of the wheat.

Russia's Infrastructure and Ranking

The World Economic Forum ranks countries for their infrastructure. Russia ranks very low on **road quality, technological adaptation,** and **burden of government regulation.**

Of the 141 countries ranked, Russia ranks in the bottom one-third in soundness of banks, its high homicide rate, the condition of transportation infrastructure, and private property rights.

The graph below compares the ranking of Russia with the United States, China, Germany, and Israel in eight categories. We have included Israel because 15% of its population, or 1.2 million people, are Russian emigrants.

3.19 Infrastructure Ranking, World Economic Forum, Major Countries

Country	Soundness of Banks	Homicide Rate	Transport Infrastructure	Utility Infrastructure	Property Rights	Skills of Current Workforce	Entrepreneurial Culture	Research and Development
Russia	115	114	113	50	113	49	77	23
U.S	25	96	12	23	30	5	2	3
China	93	15	24	65	43	37	34	10
Germany	64	33	7	24	30	16	9	2
Israel	16	47	26	13	29	17	1	16

Source: Global Competitiveness Report 2019

Russia's GDP and Economy in 2022

The Russian magazine *The Bell* has released a new update for Russian economic prospects for 2022.

The forecast calls for a fall of Russian GDP and the growth of inflation. The Bank of Russia has projected a decline in GDP of 8.0% (the highest since 1998) and inflation at 20.0%. One week after the start of the "special military operation," inflation accelerated by a multiple of four.

The European Bank for Reconstruction and Development (EBRD) projects a shrinkage of the Russian economy by 10% and Ukraine's by 20% in 2023.

To combat the effects of inflation on the population, Russia has increased pension funding and an adjustment in the price of drugs and medical goods. Russia has also adjusted the rules of admission to Russian higher educational establishments for Russians who have had to stop their education abroad due to the actions of foreign states.

Russia will regard U.S. and other nations' companies that have ceased doing business in Russia as performing a "deliberate bankruptcy" and could have criminal verdicts imposed upon them in addition to huge fines.

In its update, EBRD said North African countries were "greatly exposed" to the reduced global supply of wheat from Russia and Ukraine. It also warned that Central Asian economies that are heavily dependent on remittances from Russia have been badly hit by the fall in the value of the ruble and restrictions on its convertibility.

In addition, tourism is expected to take a hit in a number of countries including Armenia, Estonia, Georgia, and Montenegro.

Assuming the Ukraine invasion will subside in 2023, it may take Russia and Ukraine decades to recover from the economic damages.

The Russian Military

Accurate data on Russia's military forces is difficult to obtain, but here are a few statistics from the *Moscow Times*:

- In 2018, corruption in Russia's military quadrupled.

- More than 2,800 Russian military officials were brought to justice for corruption in 2018.

- Russia has dropped further in a corruption index annually compiled by Transparency International Watchdog, tying with such countries as Mexico and Lebanon.

- And this from an article in *Politico*:

- Early in the invasion of Ukraine, soldiers received rations that had expired in 2015.

- The quality of food and housing in the Russian military is reportedly worse than in its prisons.

- Russian advances in the Ukraine were slowed by lack of fuel—despite being a country that is rich with oil and gas.

- Corruption in defense procurement manifested in soldiers receiving inadequate equipment and supplies, slowing down the advancement of troops, undermining their morale, and hindering military effectiveness.

- Ukrainians have been shocked at the lack of maintenance in captured Russian military equipment.

And finally, a quote from former Russian Foreign Minister Andrei Kozyrev: "Much of the military budget was stolen and spent on mega-yachts in Cyprus. But as a military advisor you cannot report that to the president, so they reported lies to him instead."

And at this point in time, after a year of war, the results of the Ukraine invasion remain a great unknown.

3.20 Ukraine

Closing this section is a quote from Victoria Nuland of the Brookings Institution:

"Putin's failure to invest in Russia's modernization may be catching up with him. Putin's insistence on tight state control and the renationalization of key sectors of the economy has suppressed innovation and diversification. Russia's roads, rails, schools, and hospitals are crumbling. Corruption remains rampant and Russia's purchasing power continues to shrink."

Last year, a survey by the Levada Center showed that **a staggering 53% of 18- to 24-year-olds said they wanted to emigrate**. Liberal elites and educated young people continue to leave the country in droves.

Paucity of Household Goods Demand

And finally, Russia's decline in population means a continual decline in demand for household goods and housing—two categories that in growing societies drive the economies to greater success.

A concluding thought by Fellows Fiona Hill and Angela Stent:

"During his reign (1682-1725), Tsar Peter the Great opened a window to the West by traveling to Europe, inviting Europeans to come to Russia and help develop its economy. Quasi-Tsar Putin has slammed the window shut on that possibility."

On balance, the future of Russia is not bright, either demographically or economically. Its population will continue to decline and its finances will continue to hinge on high oil and wheat prices.

CHAPTER 4

A Changing China: One from Column A and One from Column B

When I was growing up, going out for foreign food meant Chinese. And you had your choice: Mandarin or Szechwan. Today, when our family goes out to dine, the entire panoply of the Far East gives us a remarkable variety of options, including Vietnamese, Thai, Indian, Japanese, and Korean, to name just a few.

And that is a severe Chinese problem. China, in years past, has been our near sole source of manufactured goods, blanketing the shelves of Walmart and Target and every grocery store. That picture is changing rapidly as China now finds itself with severe competition from countries with much lower manufacturing and operating costs. Pointedly, the other countries have learned to out-China China in terms of their manufacturing and marketing capabilities. And that means that China has to find other ways to keep its people working.

And that is only one of China's major problems. Perhaps the least mentioned, but exceptionally important, is the demographic conundrum that faces the 1.4 billion-person nation.

This report is segmented into six sections:

Section 1: Population and Quality of Life Changes
Section 2: The Education in China
Section 3: The Economy of China

Section 4. The Hour of Power
Section 5: What's the Bad News
Section 6: Wrap-up

SECTION I: POPULATION AND QUALITY OF LIFE CHANGES

A little history: In 1948, as it was recovering from World War II, China had 540 million persons and an exceptionally high birthrate. By 1980, the population almost doubled to 950 million. And the life expectancy increased from 35 years in 1948 to 66 years in 1980, an increase of 89%.

4.1 Snapshot China Growth
Population and Life Expectancy, 1948–1980

Category	1948	1980	Change	Percent Change
Population	540,000,000	950,000,000	410,000,000	76%
Life Expectancy	35	66	31	89%

Source: United Nations

4.2 Births Per Woman (Ages 18–45)
China, 1948–1980

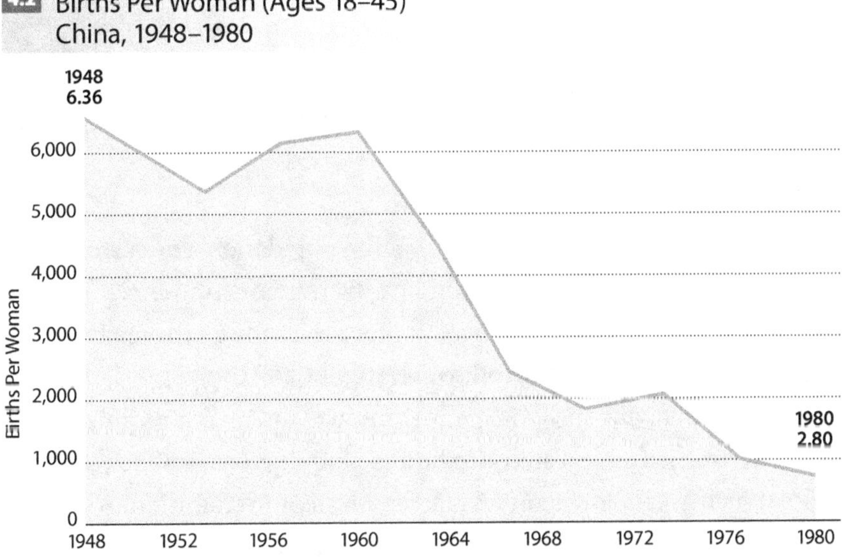

Source: United Nations Population Division

China began promoting the use of **birth control** and **family planning** with the establishment of the **People's Republic in 1949**, though such efforts remained sporadic and voluntary until after the death of Mao Zedong in 1976.

At that point, the government needed to slow down population growth because they had neither the food nor jobs to support this burgeoning population; hence, in 1980, China invoked the infamous **one-child policy**.

On **September 25, 1980**, a public letter—published by the Central Committee of the Chinese Communist Party to the party membership—called upon all to adhere to the one-child policy, and that date has often been cited as the policy's "official" start date.

The law of unintended consequences has now come home to roost.

The one-child policy produced consequences beyond the goal of reducing population growth.

As in most non-industrialized nations, male children are much favored over female children due to their manual labor prowess. Thus, when most families were restricted to one child, having a girl became highly undesirable, resulting in a rise in abortions of female fetuses and increases in the number of female children who were placed in orphanages or were abandoned.

The result: China's millennial population consists of more males than females. And that means the number of household formations has been very modest.

The one child policy ended in 2016.

Because of the low birthrates, an aging population, and a shrinking workforce, in May 2021, the Chinese government announced that all married couples would be allowed to have as many as **three children**; this was formally **passed into law in August 2021**.

Noteworthy with this change was the accompanying promise from the government that it would also be enacting supportive policy changes in areas such as employment, finance, childcare, and education to address the social and economic reasons why couples had thus far hesitated to have more children.

THE LONGER-TERM EFFECT OF THE ONE-CHILD POLICY

Demographically speaking, China has an ongoing population problem. It is projected that from 2020 to 2060 China will **decline** in population by 124,000,000 persons. In that same timeframe, the U.S. is projected to add 79 million.

A major part of the U.S. growth will depend on continued immigration. Conversely, immigration to China is meager. It has not been a warm, welcoming country.

4.3 Population (In Millions), Major Countries, 2020–2060 (Projected)

Country	2020	2060	2020–2060	
			Change	Percent Change
United States	325,700	404,500	78,800	24%
Viet Nam	103,808	121,833	18,025	17%
South Korea	51,245	46,900	(4,345)	–8%
Russia	142,021	126,898	(15,123)	–11%
European Union	448,825	432,470	(16,355)	–4%
Japan	127,141	99,100	(28,041)	–22%
China	**1,410,539**	**1,286,294**	**(124,245)**	**–9%**

Source: United Nations Population Division

The aging of the Chinese population is best shown in these two graphs, prepared by author Peter Zeihan. In 1990, the graph shows a population bulge in the under-40-year-old range:

4.4 China Demography, 1990

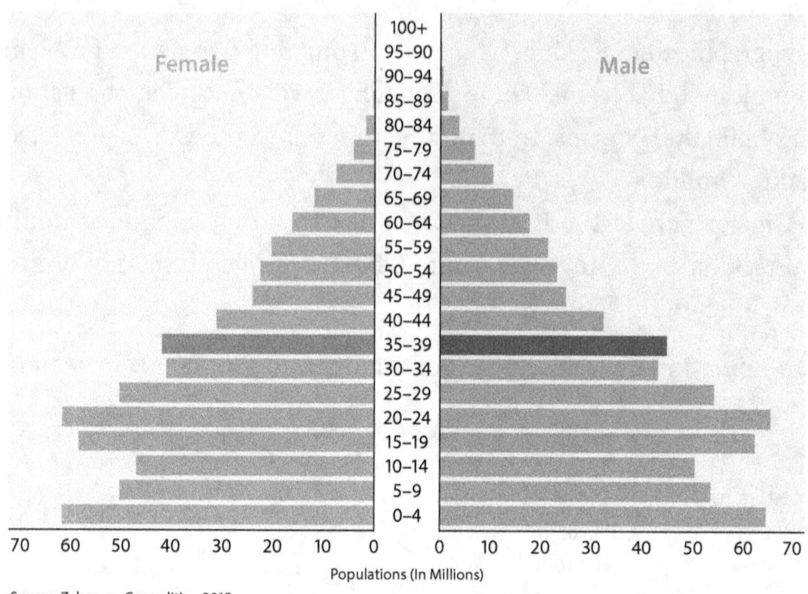

Source: Zehan on Geopolitics, 2015

Fast-forward 20 years, and the bulge moves up dramatically with most population additions in the **over-40-year-old** category:

4.5 China Demography, 2040

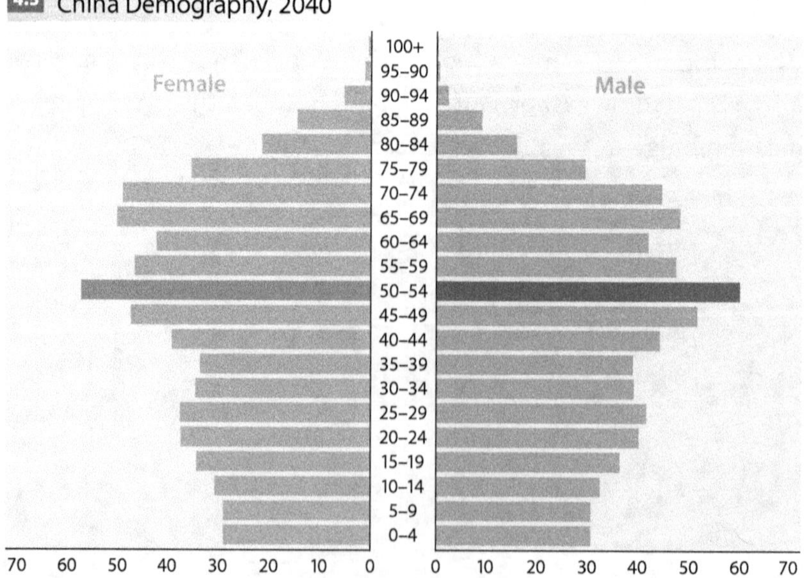

Source: Zehan on Geopolitics, 2015

The increase in the percentage of the population over age 65 in China has moved upward in a highly aggressive manner, from 5.7% in 1990 to a projected 24% in 2040.

4.6 Percent of Population over Age 65
Major Countries, 1990–2040 (Projected)

Country	1990	2020	2040
Japan	11.9	26.6	34
South Korea	5.2	13	31
European Union	12.7	19.4	26
China	**5.7**	**10.1**	**24**
United States	12.6	14.9	22
Russia	10.3	13.6	20
India	3.8	6	11

Source: United Nations Population Division

This exhibit summarizes the World Bank projections of population, population under age 18, and the fertility rate of several major countries. Perhaps most poignant is that in China **the number of persons under age 18 has declined from 43% of the population to 21% of the population.**

4.7 Comparison of Major Countries, Population and Fertility Factors

Factor	United States	India	China	Russia	Japan
Population					
2020	1,510,082,000	223,852,000	347,908,000	82,293,000	142,227,000
2050	363,794,358	37,769,000	48,840,589	1,596,386	(662,869)
Change	**(1,146,287,642)**	**(186,083,000)**	**(299,067,411)**	**(80,696,614)**	**(142,889,869)**
Percent Change	–76%	–83%	–86%	–98%	–100%
1980	27%	46%	25%	35%	0%
2020	0%	0%	0%	0%	0%
Fertility					
1980	1.49	5.65	1.55	2.03	1.68
2020	0.00	0.00	0.00	0.00	0.00

Source: World Bank, International Monetary Fund

The effect of these phenomena has been predictable:

The paucity of household formations means that the dollars spent on new housing, household goods, and the myriad of goods that forming households normally acquire in the millennial years has not been sufficient to keep the Chinese manufacturing machine going, which means that the labor force is aging and less productive and less adventurous in accepting new manufacturing and scientific methodologies. Not good for China.

Immigration

For countries with lackluster birthrates, immigration can be a saving grace. For countries like India, Russia, and China, immigration is not a popular option.

4.8 Immigration by Country, Six Major Nations, 2021

Country	Total Population	Net Migration	Immigration as Percent of Population
India	1,380,004,000	(2,663,000)	–0.193%
China	1,439,324,000	(1,742,000)	–0.121%
Russia	145,934,000	106,000	0.073%
United States	331,003,000	477,000	0.144%
Germany	83,240,000	208,000	0.250%
Great Britain	67,215,000	270,000	0.402%

Source: Moody's Analytics; World Bank

Human Development Index

The Human Development Index (HDI) is **a summary measure of human development.** It measures the average achievements in a country in three basic dimensions of human development: a **long and healthy life, being knowledgeable, and having a decent standard of living. Note China's standing in the HDI.**

4.9 Human Development Index
Survey: 154 Countries, World Bank/UNESCO

Country	Human Development Index (HDI) Value	Life Expectancy at Birth Years	Expected Years of Schooling Years	Mean Years of Schooling Years	Gross National Income (GNI) per Capita 2017 PPP $	HDI Rank
United States	0.926	78.9	16.3	13.4	63,826	17
Russia	0.824	72.6	15.0	12.2	26,157	49
China	0.761	76.9	14.0	8.1	16,057	80
India	0.645	69.7	12.2	6.5	6,681	130

Source: World Bank/UNESCO

SECTION 2: EDUCATION IN CHINA

China's enormous patent achievements and its remarkable output of goods of all qualities could not take place without a very strong education system.

On the education front, China has made major strides in the past few decades, **almost doubling the level of educational attainment since 1980**. Of the major nations, only India has achieved a more rigorous achievement.

4.10 Education Attainment
Selected Countries, 1980–2015

Country	1980	2000	2015	Change 1980–2015	Percent Change
China	**0.136**	**0.227**	**0.263**	**0.127**	**93%**
India	0.073	0.132	0.201	0.128	176%
Japan	0.492	0.691	0.656	0.165	33%
Russia	0.343	0.364	0.597	0.253	74%
USA	0.586	0.746	0.787	0.201	34%

Source. United Nations AHDI ratings

Education scoring depends to a major degree on the government's expenditures on education. In this exhibit, we show the change in expenditures for public education for selected counties. China has made major progress in that category, moving upward from 72% to 126% in six years:

These next two exhibits show the major increase in educational attainment in the younger age groups in China. In Exhibit 4.12, the percent of the **25- to 64-year-old** population with a bachelor's or a master's degree is negligible.

But, when you look at the more youthful population, ages **25-34,** the percent of graduation for both men and women rises very significantly to 18%. It is still significantly below the percentage of the other nations in the exhibit, but it does show major strides for China. Pointedly, the younger Chinese population has a far higher level of education than the older Chinese population.

4.11 Index of Change, Total Public Expenditure on Education, 2012 and 2018

Nation	2012	2018
China	72%	126%
Korea	93%	112%
Japan	100%	101%
U.S.	99%	107%
Germany	98%	107%
India	82%	121%

Source: OECD

4.12 Level of Education Adults 25–64 as of 2020

Nation	Bachelor's	Master's
China	3%	0%
Korea	32%	40%
Japan	31%	9%
U.S.	25%	12%
Germany	17%	12%
India	9%	9%

Source: OECD

4.13 College Graduation, Men and Women Adults 25–34 as of 2020

Nation	Men	Women
China	18%	18%
Korea	66%	61%
Japan	59%	64%
U.S.	47%	57%
Germany	33%	36%
India	22%	17%

Source: OECD

SECTION 3: THE ECONOMY OF CHINA

This chapter focuses on the economy of China.

The basis for China's economy is displayed in this chart:

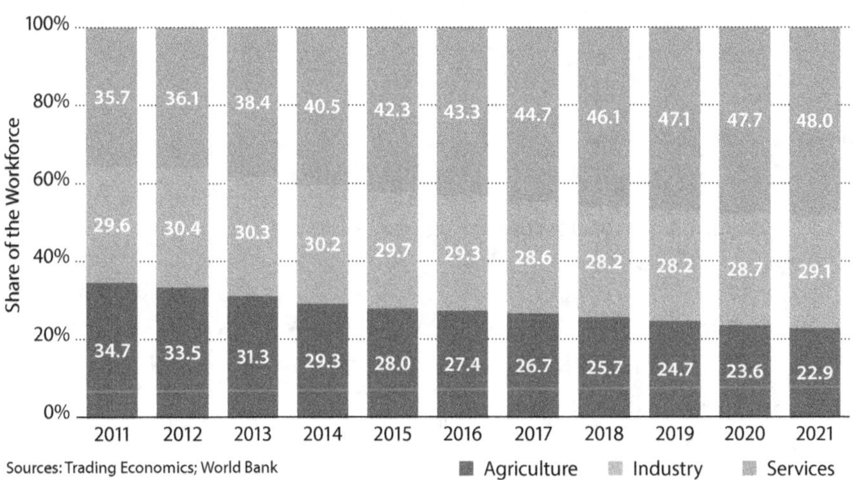

In the past decade, the percent of employment devoted to agriculture has declined dramatically from 34.7% to 22.9%—symbolic of the increasing industrialization of the country. In the U.S., only 4.0% of employment is devoted to agriculture.

The percent devoted to industrial production has remained stable, but service employment has increased substantially, recognizing that the servicing is providing service to increasingly educated and affluent Chinese citizens.

China remains the world's largest supplier of manufactured goods, producing almost twice the percentage as the United States.

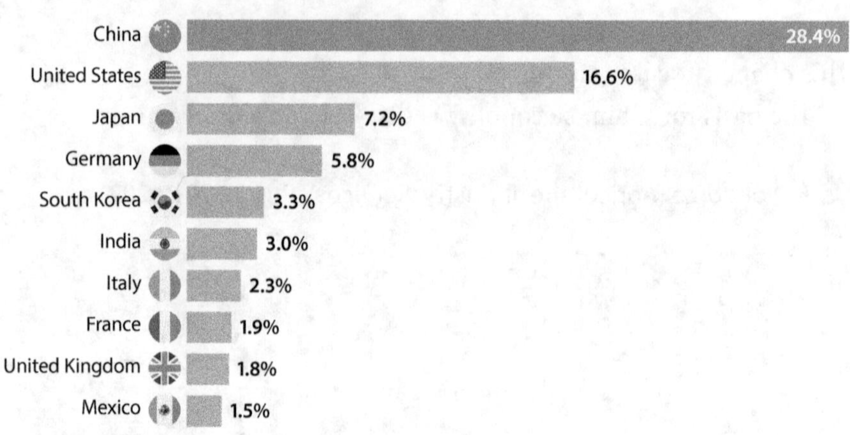

4.15 Manufacturing Output (Value Added Basis[1])

1. Output measured on a value-added basis in current U.S. dollars

Source: United Nations Statistics Division

In terms of billions of dollars, China, Hong Kong, South Korea, and Japan together, in 2021, produced three times the output of the U.S.

4.16 Exports from the Far East, 2021

Country	Billions of Dollars, U.S.
China	$3,363.00
Japan	$756.00
Hong Kong	$669.00
South Korea	$644.00
Total	$5,432.00

4.17 Leading Export Countries Worldwide (In Billions of Dollars), 2021

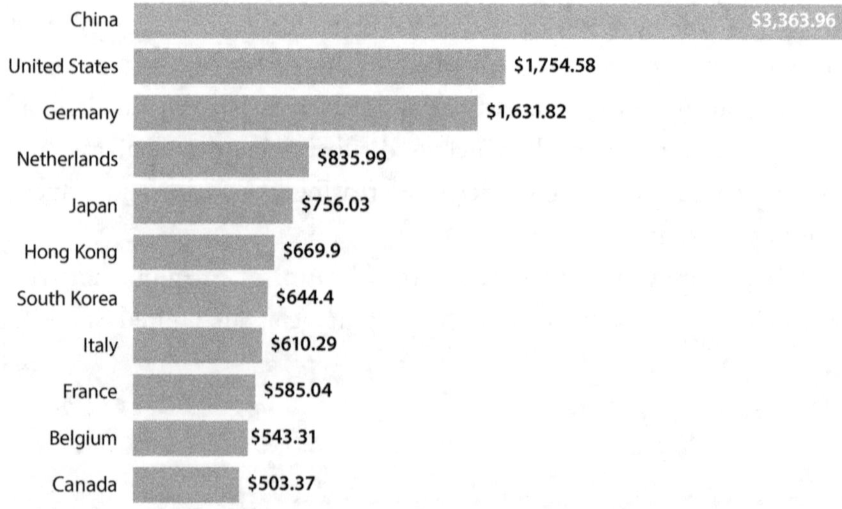

The exhibit below shows the billions of dollars of exports to the U.S. in the past decade:

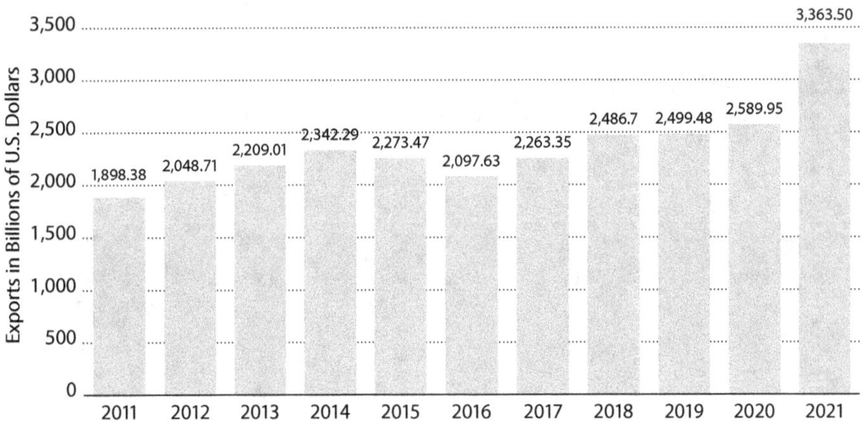

4.18 Value of Export of Goods from China (In Billions of Dollars) 2011–2021

Gross National Product

Gross National Product (GNP) is the sum of all goods and services produced by a country. It's a measuring stick that is calculated by several sophisticated organizations and tends to be accurate even for Third World countries.

The world is about to pass the $100 trillion mark.

4.19 World GNP in Billions, 2016–2021

Year	Billions	U.S. Percent
2016	76,439	1.0%
2017	81,359	1.1%
2018	86,347	1.1%
2019	87,607	1.2%
2020	84,705	1.1%
2021	89,702	1.2%
2022[1]	94,097	1.2%

1. Based on first 3 quarters

Source: World Bank

Looking back 50 years, China accounted for three-fourths of 1.0% of the world's GNP. Fast Forward to 2020 and a remarkable story reveals itself. In that 50-year period, China has moved into **second place** with one-sixth of the world's GNP. And note that California is moving up, but probably won't catch up to China in our lifetime.

4.20 Gross Domestic Product (Trillions of Dollars)
Major Countries, A 50-Year Pictrure, 1970–2020

Country	1970	Percentage of World	2020	Percentage of World
World	**$12.14**	**100.00%**	**$87.70**	**100.00%**
United States	$1.07	**8.84%**	$21.43	**24.44%**
China	$0.09	**0.76%**	$14.34	**16.35%**
Japan	$0.21	1.70%	$5.08	5.79%
Germany	$0.20	1.67%	$3.86	4.40%
California	$0.11	0.91%	$3.30	**3.76%**
India	$0.06	0.51%	$2.87	3.27%
United Kingdom	$0.12	1.01%	$2.83	3.23%
Russia	$0.21	1.70%	$1.70	1.94%
South Korea	$0.08	0.66%	$1.65	1.88%
Mexico	$0.04	0.32%	$1.27	1.45%

Sources: World Bank, Directorate of Intelligence, CIA

On a **per capita basis**, the **U.S. has an average GDP six times that of China;** however, given the ongoing strengths of the China economy, that six times will be trimmed to two times by 2040.

4.21 Gross Domestic Product Per Capita
Major Countries, 2000–2040 (Projected)

Country	2000[1]	2020[2]	2040[3]	2000–2020		2020–2040	
				Change	Percent Change	Change	Percent Change
United States	$36,449	$67,082	$75,700	30,633	84%	8,618	13%
China	$959	$10,971	$34,000	10,012	1044%	23,029	210%
Japan	$38,532	$42,748	$58,200	4,216	11%	15,452	36%
European Union	$19,740	$36,593	$40,848	16,853	85%	4,255	12%
South Korea	$11,947	$34,209	$58,600	22,262	186%	24,391	71%
Russia	$1,771	$11,710	$44,800	9,939	561%	33,090	283%
India	438	2379	18300	1941	0.443	15921	0.669
Ratio		6.11	2.23				

Source: 1. World Bank; 2. International Monetary Fund; 3. European Commission (Global Europe 2050)

On a household basis, the U.S. median income per capita is $19,306, five times that of the household income in China ($4,246).

Forty percent of China's population—some 600 million people—earn an average of about $140 per month.

4.22 Median Household Income
Per Capita, Major Countries, 2021

Country	2021
United States	$19,306
Canada	$18,652
Germany	$16,845
United Kingdom	$14,793
Japan	$14,543
South Korea	$12,507
Russia	$5,504
China	$4,246
Mexico	$3,315
India	$1,314

Source: World Bank, United Nation

Tax Collections

The economic growth of China can be seen in their tax collections over the past decade. On average, their **collection increases have averaged more than 18% per annum.**

4.23 Tax Collections, China, 2010–2020

Category	In Billions			Percent Change	Annual Percent Change
	2010	2020	Change		
Total Tax Revenue	$7,321	$20,340	$13,019	178%	8.9%
Taxes on Income	$1,896	$5,446	$3,550	187%	9.4%
Taxes on Property	$540	$1,505	$965	179%	8.9%
Taxes on Goods and Services	$4,805	$8,476	$3,671	76%	3.8%
Enterprise Income Tax	$1,284	$3,643	$2,359	184%	9.2%

Source: Organization for Economic Co-Operation and Development (OCED)

Patent Power

The World Intellectual Property Organization tracks the **patent activity** worldwide, but particularly what it calls GIH (**Global Innovation Hotspots**). In its most recent index,

4.24 Patents
Global Innovation Hotspots, 1991–1995 and 2011–2015

Global Innovation Hotspot	1991–1995	2011–2015
China	42.3	60.3
Germany	63.8	63.5
Japan	51.5	56.3
U.S.	30.8	36.5

Source: WIPO

China had the strongest gains in patents of any First World country:

Looking at the patents in recent decades, China had scant activity in the 1970-1989 period but has **expanded tenfold** since then. In fact, in 2018, China's intellectual property office received a record 4.54 million patent applications **(half the world's total)**.

4.25 Patent Power Tilts to Asia, 1970–2018

Nation	Share of Patents		
	1970–1979	1980–1989	2000–2018
China	1.0%	1.0%	10.0%
Japan	21.0%	29.0%	24.0%
United States	28.0%	24.0%	22.0%
Germany	12.0%	16.0%	11.0%

Source: World Intellectual Property Organization

SECTION 4: THE HOUR OF POWER

For China to produce its enormous number of products and to provide heating, air conditioning, and cooking power to its 1.4 billion population, the country must generate an enormous amount of energy.

Fortunately for China, it is one of four countries that is saturated with coal (Russia, the U.S., and Australia). **It's the world's largest consumer, producer, and importer of coal, with its consumption and production each accounting for around half of the world's total.**

According to China's National Bureau of Statistics, coal accounted for 50% of the country's energy consumption in 2021. Notably, that is a reduction from 70% in the mid-2000s.

Over the past 40 years, China has had an annual GNP growth of 9.5% on average. Only by using a low-cost fuel like coal could the country support its economic growth.

China produces about 90% of the coal it consumes, but it imports about 70% of its oil and 50% of its gas needs.

China appears to be serious about cutting back its coal use, but in the first few weeks of 2022, it announced that five new coal power projects had been approved; however, the country announced that it will not build any new coal-fired projects abroad.

China appears to be serious about cutting back its coal use. Time will tell. Meanwhile, incidents of lung diseases have caused the cost of healthcare to rise dramatically.

SECTION 5: WHAT'S THE BAD NEWS

Obviously, the economy of China is a modern miracle, but there are a few items that deserve mention that are not inspiring:

Leadership and Control

In many respects, we need China and China needs us. The President of China, Xi Jinping, is not our enemy. In fact, he speaks perfectly good English and his daughter graduated Harvard. How bad can he be? The question arises: **How long can he be the president?** Politically, he can rule forever, but he is 70 years old, overweight, and smokes heavily.

China is a one-person-ruled country where that one person makes all the rules and has the power to enforce them. There's no congress, no senate, no supreme court, no governors—just Xi Jinping. Xi doesn't welcome feedback.

Cost of Production

A key problem is that producing goods in China has become increasingly expensive. It no longer is the Third World country that can provide the world with cheap goods. It now has competition from Third World countries.

Labor Shortage

Because of Russia's labor shortage, a substantial part of their farm employment is Chinese. Currently, the Chinese farm 1,300 square miles of Russian land in eastern Russia.

Potential Control over Other Countries

Many countries, like Germany, sell many billions of dollars in goods to China. And China wants to invest more in Germany including a major transportation project. China is in a very good position to cause economic havoc with Germany and others like it by investing heavily in those countries.

Chinese Lending

The Chinese use lending as a weapon to dominate Third World countries.

Human Rights Abuse

There are some 2.0 million-plus Turkish-speaking Uyghurs (Muslims) living in China's Xinjiang region (far northwest China) in camps and subject to reeducation. Another 9.0 million are suffering from a crackdown by Chinese authorities. Stories abound of torture, sleep deprivation, children moved to orphanages, and women being raped. Apparently, China wants them to renounce their religion.

Hong Kong

Hong Kong used to be a thriving place to live and work. But the bullies in China's government insist on ruining it.

COVID

Most certainly, China did not want to become the center or founder of COVID, but it did, and the virus proceeded to cause 6.5 million-plus deaths worldwide.

Geology

If China has one overwhelming long-term problem, it is geological. It is surrounded by countries that are not warm and fuzzy, and certainly these neighbors do nothing to strengthen China and do not want to be business partners with it (though they have no choice). The map below visually displays China's geologic problem.

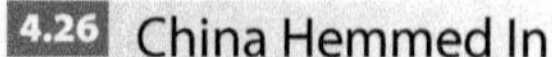

4.26 China Hemmed In

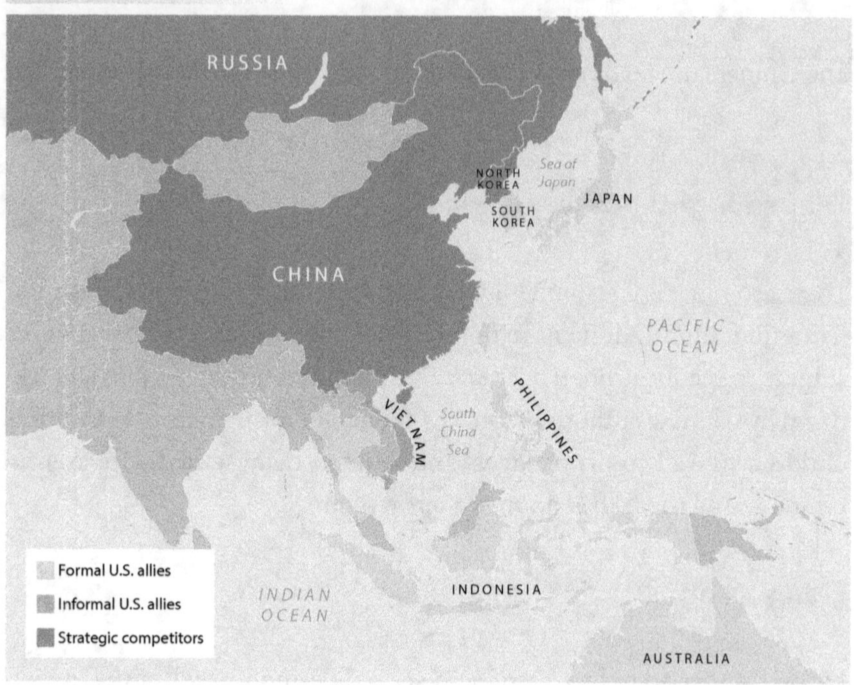

Coastal Crowding

China is the same size as the United States (in terms of square miles), but its population is heavily crowded into the area facing the East China Sea.

China is an enormous country, in terms of acreage, but its populace wants to live in the big cities where the jobs are. That means incredible crowding near the waterfront cities and the possibilities for raging illnesses. And perpetually dark skies as the coal fires burn.

4.27 China

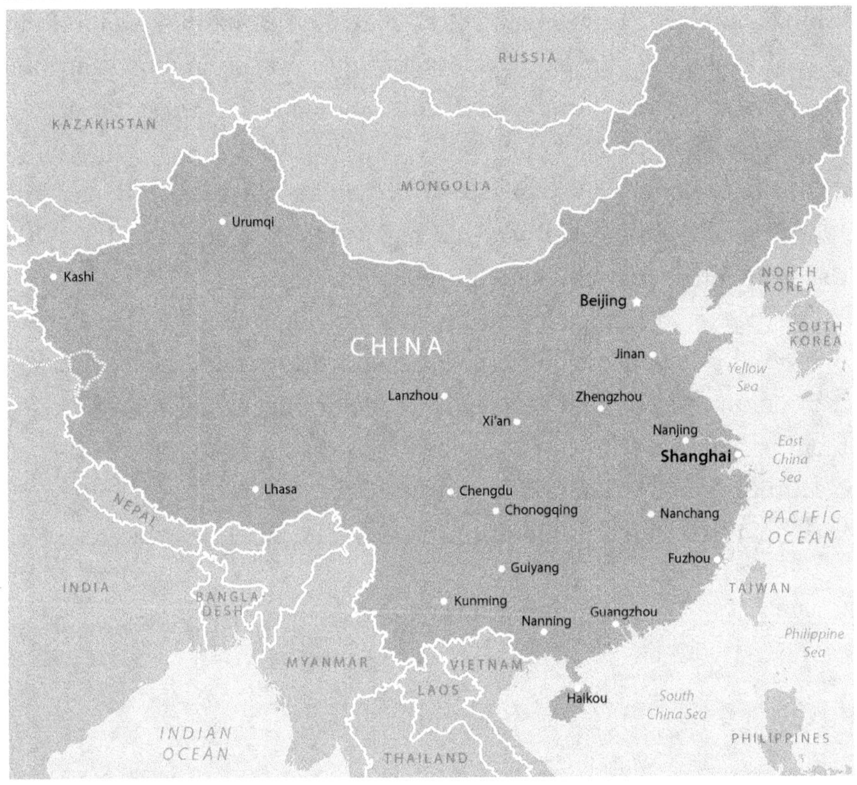

RUSSIA
KAZAKHSTAN
MONGOLIA
Urumqi
Kashi
NORTH KOREA
Beijing
SOUTH KOREA
CHINA
Jinan
Yellow Sea
Lanzhou
Zhengzhou
Xi'an
Nanjing
East China Sea
Shanghai
Lhasa
Chengdu
NEPAL
Chonogqing
Nanchang
PACIFIC OCEAN
Fuzhou
INDIA
Guiyang
BANGLA DESH
TAIWAN
Kunming
Guangzhou
Philippine Sea
MYANMAR
Nanning
VIETNAM
LAOS
Haikou
South China Sea
PHILIPPINES
INDIAN OCEAN
THAILAND

SECTION 6: THE WRAP-UP

China is a miracle in the making. It is a nation that has figured out how to feed 1.4 billion people, provide them with clothing and housing and jobs, and at the same time manufacture enough goods to be the largest supplier in the world.

The entire miracle of China did not happen in a democratic fashion. It never could. It took a military-like regime many decades to accomplish the rising prosperity and an educated workforce.

Yes, there were hiccups along the way, like the now abandoned one-child rule and the COVID disaster. It has shown the world that it can dramatically enhance education, be highly inventive, and use its seemingly endless funds to acquire lands and goods production in a multitude of countries around the world.

China isn't warm and fuzzy, but it is a miracle in the making.

CHAPTER 5

India: The World's Largest Democracy

Prior to delving into the economy and demographics of India, I thought it would be beneficial to display its location in the world:

5.1 India in the World

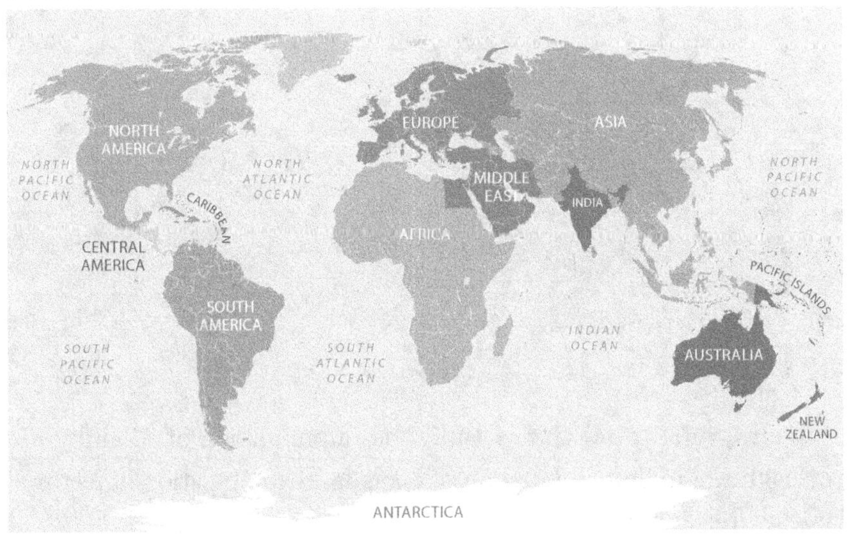

Here's a close-up of India, noting its three largest metropolitan areas:

5.2 India

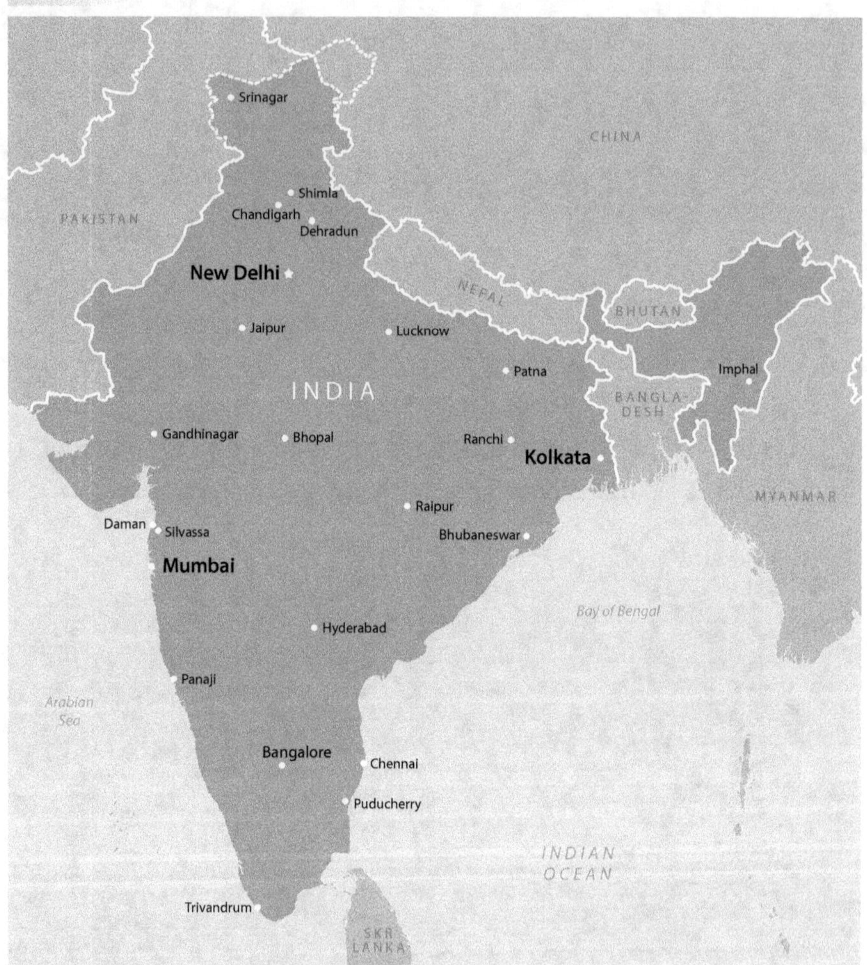

Delhi, the capital city of India, has a population of 31 million—versus the 38 million population of Canada. The population of its three largest cities is shown here:

5.3 Major Metropolitan Areas — India 2011–2021

Area	Millions			
	2011	2021	Change	% Change
Mumbai (Bombay)	18.3	20.8	2.5	14%
Dehli	16.3	31.3	15.0	92%
Kolkata (Calcutta)	14.0	18.5	4.5	32%

As an aside, in 1950, there was only one city in the world with more than 10 million people (New York). Now there are 33. So sayeth the United Nations.

SECTION 1: THE DEMOGRAPHICS OF INDIA

Background on modern India: Prime Minister Pandit Nehru was enamored with socialism as practiced in the USSR, and therefore his great emphasis was on public-sector rather than private-sector investment. Following the USSR model, he pursued heavy steel production with a very limited investment in education or the sciences.

Conversely, China started with assembly in the first stage, component production in the second stage, manufacturing of machinery to produce components in the third stage, and then machines to produce machines in the fourth stage. This approach not only generated employment to start with but also started the industrialization process in a meaningful way.

As a result, the Indian population continued to be dependent on agriculture in the 1950s and 1960s, and in those decades there was essentially no reduction in poverty. In the 1990s the Nehru model was abandoned. And only then did India begin to undertake major investments in education and the sciences.

There are five mega-countries that are the primary providers of goods and services for the world: the U.S., China, the European Union (which is 28 countries combined), Russia, and India.

The U.S. and China are obvious because of their enormous production capabilities. Russia remains in the top five because it is a First World country with a highly educated population and major exports (oil, aeronautics, and grain), although this status has been threatened and diminished by the Ukrainian war.

India lags behind and can still be categorized as a Second World country, but with over 1.4 billion people and a strong work ethic, it will, in time, move into First World status.

Of the five, only the U.S. and India are anticipated to gain population during the next 30 years. The European Union, Russia, and China will gradually lose their population base.

Pointedly, India will add a **quarter billion population** in the next 30 years.

5.4 Population Projection, Major Countries, 2020–2050

Country	2020	2050	Change 2020–2050	
			Number	Percent
India	1,380,000,000	1,639,176,000	259,176,000	19%
United States	331,003,000	379,419,000	48,416,000	15%
European Union – 29 countries	446,825,000	441,200,000	(5,625,000)	–1%
Russia	145,934,000	135,824,000	(10,110,000)	–7%
China	1,439,324,000	1,402,405,000	(36,919,000)	–3%

Source: United Nations Department of Economic and Social Affairs, Population Division

The U.S. gain in population will substantially be due to in-migration while India's will be the result of natural household formation (i.e.,

5.5 Fertility (Children Per Woman) Major Countries, 1990–2040 (Projected)

Country	1990	2020	2040
India	**3.81**	**2.10**	**1.80**
United States	3.03	1.84	1.83
China	2.21	1.45	1.56
Russia	1.87	1.60	1.60

Source: United Nations

more children). Having said that, it is important to note that India's fertility rate has moved downward in the past 30 years and may equal that of the United States by 2040.

Nonetheless, India's "under age 19" population will ensure its population growth for many decades.

5.6 Percent of Population Under Age 19 Major Countries, 1990–2040 (Projected)

Country	1990	2020	2040
India	**47%**	**36%**	**28%**
United States	29%	25%	23%
China	26%	21%	21%
European Union	38%	20%	11%
Russia	30%	23%	6%

Source: United Nations Population Division

Stage of Human Development

With the exception of China, India's immediate neighbors (Bangladesh, Nepal, and Pakistan) are among the least developed countries in the world. Of the 188 countries in the United Nations' **Human Development Index**, these three are in the bottom quarter.

**5.7 Human Development Index
India and Its Neighbors**

Country	Human Development Index (HDI)	Life Expectancy at Birth	Expected Years of Schooling	Mean Years of Schooling	Gross National Income (GNI) per Capita	HDI Rank
	Value	Years	Years	Years	2017 PPP $	
India	**0.645**	**69.7**	**12.2**	**6.5**	**$6,681**	**130**
Bangladesh	0.632	72.6	11.6	6.2	$4,976	134
Nepal	0.602	70.8	12.8	5.0	$3,457	143
Pakistan	0.557	67.3	8.3	5.2	$5,005	154
China	0.761	76.9	14.0	8.1	$16,057	80

Total countries in survey: 188

Source: UNESCO

India's population is 80% Hindu, 13% Muslim, 2% Sikh, 2% Christian, and 3% other minorities. These divisions have historically caused tensions between different religious groups.

Hindi and English are India's official languages, but there are also 17 regional languages that are considered official.

SECTION 2: THE ECONOMICS OF INDIA

"Economists have long recognized that productivity per worker is the best indicator of a country's average standard of living and overall economic power. The higher a country's productivity, the higher the average household income and the higher the population's material well-being will be."

—Matthew J. Slaughter, Dartmouth College

Further, the higher a country's productivity, the larger the country's overall tax base, channeling more funds to the government for national defense, education, care of the aged, and other interests.

A country can raise its level of productivity by investing in the capital used to create things, or it can create new ideas. **Innovation** has long driven the United States' rising productivity—accounting for well over half the U.S. per capita GDP growth over the past century. India, not so much.

There are two basic ways that a country can raise its **level of productivity**:

1. improve or invent capital goods (i.e., machinery) and
2. data-driven innovations.

Capital goods require an enormous amount of money to propel a country into a strong competitive position. Conversely, **data-driven innovations** require only brainpower, education, and access to computers.

Access to data has been revolutionizing science, medicine, and communications, among other things. The supply of data is endless, readily available, and cheap.

Think in terms of what has been accomplished in a relatively short timeframe because of the computer and data availability: the Human Genome Project; COVID vaccines, social media (Alphabet, Facebook, TikTok,) and Amazon.

India is a country with substantial brainpower and access to data. It has made remarkable strides in terms of gross domestic product (GDP) in the past 30 years. GDP is the sum of all the goods and services produced by a country. **Since 1990, India has increased its GDP more than eight times:**

5.8 Gross Domestic Product (Millions) India, 1990–2020

Year	GDP	Change from Previous Years	Percent Annual Change
1990	$320,979		
2000	$468,395	$147,416	4.6%
2010	$1,675,620	$1,207,225	25.8%
2020	$2,667,690	$992,070	7.4%
Change 1990–2020	**8.3**		

Source: World Bank

India's GDP gains between 1990 and 2020 are stunning, but I have looked at numerous reports by credible institutions and they all anticipate a continued major gain in the GDP of India in the next two decades.

In fact, in a recent PricewaterhouseCoopers (PwC) forecast, they anticipate that India will increase its GDP by 10 times from 2020 to 2040.

5.9 Gross Domestic Product (In Trillions)
Major Countries, 2020–2040 (Projected)

Country	2020	2040	2020–2040	
			Change	Percent Change
India	$2,597	$28,021	25,424	979%
United States	$19,390	$34,102	14,712	76%
European Union	$16,538	$21,567	5,029	30%
China	$12,237	$49,853	37,616	307%
Russia	$1,577	$5,127	3,550	225%

Source: PWC, GDP at Market Exchange Rates, February 2015; International Monetary Fund

On a **per capita** basis, India has increased its gross domestic product more than four times in the past 20 years.

5.10 Gross Domestic Product Per Capita
Major Countries, 2000–2020

Country	2000	2020	2000–2020	
India	$438	$2,379	1,941	443%
United States	$36,449	$67,082	30,633	84%
European Union	$19,740	$36,593	16,853	85%
Russia	$1,771	$11,710	9,939	561%
China	$959	$10,971	10,012	1044%

Source: PWC, GDP at Market Exchange Rates, February 2015; International Monetary Fund

Projections by the World Bank and International Monetary Fund call for India to increase its GDP per capita by almost 700% from 2020–2040 with a per capita GDP of more than $18,000 in 2040.

5.11 Gross Domestic Product Per Capita
Major Countries, 2020–2040 (Projected)

Country	2020	2040	2020–2040	
India	$2,379	$18,300	15,921	669%
United States	$67,082	$75,700	8,618	13%
European Union	$36,593	$40,848	4,255	12%
Russia	$11,710	$44,800	33,090	283%
China	$10,971	$34,000	23,029	210%

Source: World Bank, International Monetary Fund, European Commission (Global Europe 2015)

The difference between "lagging countries" and those that are moving forward is that in the lagging countries output is typically **agricultural** while the countries moving up in the world rely most on **industrialization**. India is gradually making the shift to industrialization.

Between 1990 and 2015, India moved up from 14th in the world to sixth in terms of manufacturing output.

5.12 Changes in Country Rank Ordering on Manufacturing Output
Selected Major Countries, 1990–2015

Country	1990	2015	Major Increase in Ranking	Major Decrease in Ranking
China	8	1	X	
South Korea	12	5	X	
India	14	6	X	
United States	1	2	11%	
Japan	2	3	6%	
Russia	7	15		X

Source: UN Conference on Trade and Development 2016, Brookings Institute

For instance, India is now the second-largest producer of steel in the world, outpacing every country except China.

5.13 Steel Production
Top Five Countries, 2021

Countries	Million Tons
China	1,032,790
India	118,201
Japan	98,334
United States	87,791
Russia	75,585

Source: World Steel Association

Exhibit 2.7 notes the top 10 production industries in India:

5.14 Top 10 Industries, India	
Rank	Industry
1	Iron and Steel
2	Textiles (cotton and synthetic)
3	Jute (30% of world output)
4	Sugar
5	Cement
6	Paper
7	Petrochemical
8	Automobiles
9	Information Technology (IT)
10	Banking and Insurance

Source: World Steel Association

Research and Development

India's weak spot is its expenditures on **R&D:** one of the lowest in the world at $43 per capita. India's gross expenditures on R&D as a percentage of GDP has been consistent and hovered around 0.7% for about a decade. This is even lower than Brazil (1.16%) and South Africa (0.83%). Of Second World countries, only Mexico has a lower share of R&D than India (.31%).

Despite a low expenditure on R&D, India has published more research papers than Russia and South Korea.

On average, however, the country has not performed well in the **"knowledge worker"** category: **India is "missing" its educated middle class.** The country needs considerable improvement and should push its R&D expenditures to reach **2.0%,** which would be instrumental in achieving the GDP goal of a $5.0 trillion economy by the late 2020s. This would further influence its innovative footprint across the globe.

The world map below shows India's current R&D spending as a percentage of GDP:

5.15 India's R&D Spending Compared to Other Second and First World Countries

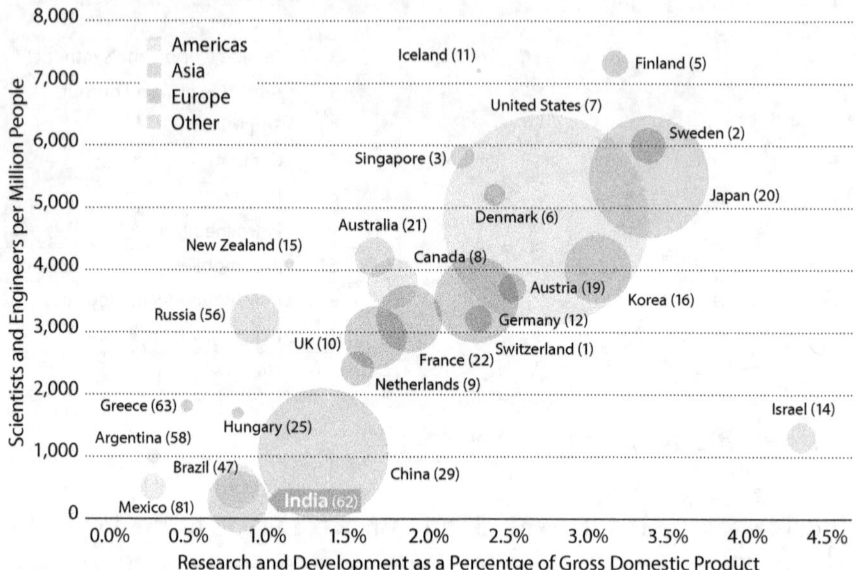

Source: R&D Magazine

The result of low R&D spending is that India has a meager record of high technology exports as a percentage of its manufactured goods. It even has less than Russia.

5.16 High-Technology Exports as Percent of Manufactured Goods, Selected Major Countries, 2010 and 2018

Country	2010	2018
China	32%	31%
United Kingdom	24%	22%
United States	23%	19%
Russia	10%	11%
India	**8%**	**9%**

High-technology exports are products with high R&D intensity such as aerospace, computers, pharmaceuticals, scientific instruments and electrical machinery.

Source: World Bank DataBank.

India's economic goal is to move forward on an aggressive basis. That goal will require a major increase in spending in R&D and education in advanced technology. India is working hard to achieve these goals.

SECTION 3: THE INDIA EDUCATION SYSTEM AND HOUSEHOLD INCOME

Though its shortfall in R&D spending ties into the education system, India is making progress.

The United Nations prepares a **Human Development Index** (HDI) each year, ranking countries on their life expectancies, education, and gross national income per capita. And then it ranks all 188 countries in the world.

In the past 30 years, India has made major strides in education as noted in this exhibit:

5.17 Change in Human Development Index, India, 1990–2020

Factor	1990	2000	2010	2020	Change 1990–2020
Life expectancy at birth	58.7	62.7	66.5	69.7	17%
Expected years of schooling	8.0	8.3	10.4	12.2	53%
Mean years of schooling	2.8	4.1	4.2	6.5	132%
Gross national income (GNI) per capita	$1,790	$2,002	$3,034	$6,681	273%
Rank	43	49	57	63	

Source: UNESCO

But compared to the U.S., Russia, and China, India has a long way to go in HDI.

5.18 Human Development Index
World Bank/UNESCO

Country	Human Development Index (HDI) Value	Life Expectancy at Birth Years	Expected Years of Schooling Years	Mean Years of Schooling Years	Gross National Income (GNI) per Capita 2017 PPP $	HDI Rank
United States	0.926	78.9	16.3	13.4	63,826	17
Russia	0.824	72.6	15.0	12.2	26,157	49
China	0.761	76.9	14.0	8.1	16,057	80
India	**0.645**	**69.7**	**12.2**	**6.5**	**6,681**	**130**

Source: World Bank/UNESCO

India has 1,043 universities, 42,343 colleges, and 11,779 stand-alone institutions, making it one of the largest higher education sectors in the world. The number of institutions has expanded by more than 400% since 2000.

However, only 2.7% of the colleges offer a Ph.D. program and only 35% run post-graduate-level programs. At the Ph.D. level, most students are enrolled in engineering, technology, and science.

In total, fewer than 10% of adults in India have a bachelor's degree or higher compared to 35% in the U.S.

In 2020, India's central government introduced a **National Education Policy** that is expected to bring profound changes to education in India.

The government allocates 4.5% of its total gross domestic product on education—a percentage smaller than most developed countries. India's current goal is to increase the public investment in education to 6.0% of its GDP. (The U.S. spends 6.0%.)

Further, India needs to heighten faculty recruitment supported by training and equipment, and send brighter students to First World countries to complete their education.

India has 350,000,000 persons younger than age 18 to educate, so it has its work cut out for it. And gender equality must be included in the educational effort.

In the short run, a steady outward migration to countries with better living standards may have left India deprived of its best talent.

Household Income

As in all countries, education levels correlate with household income.

In India, the top 1% of households have 21% of the total household income. The bottom 50% have 13% of total household income. The top 10% earn more than 20 times what the bottom 50% does.

5.19 Extreme Inequality in Income Levels

Middle 40% of the population earn 29.7% of total income

	Average Income (Rs)	Share of Total
Full Population	2,04,200	100.0%
Bottom 50%	53,610	13.1%
Top 10%	11,66,520	57.1%
Top 1%	—	21.7%

Source: World Inequality Report 2022

The good news is that, according to the government, in the past decade more than 90 million people in India rose out of extreme poverty.

A major source of household income is related to India's **tourism industry.** In 2018 more than **10 million foreign tourists** visited India. That provided 10% of India's GDP. The tourism industry provided employment for 39 million persons (8.0% of total jobs) and is projected to employ 53 million within the next decade.

As part of the tourism industry, **medical tourism**—mostly cosmetic—is growing exponentially. Medical tourism is popular because of its low cost healthcare and international standards compliance. Approximately two million patients visit India each year from 78 countries. (*Hindustan Times*)

A $150,000 open-heart surgery in the U.S. can be completed for $3,000 to $10,000 in India's best hospitals. (indiacardiacsurgerysite.com)

The exhibit below shows India's rapidly expanding middle class.

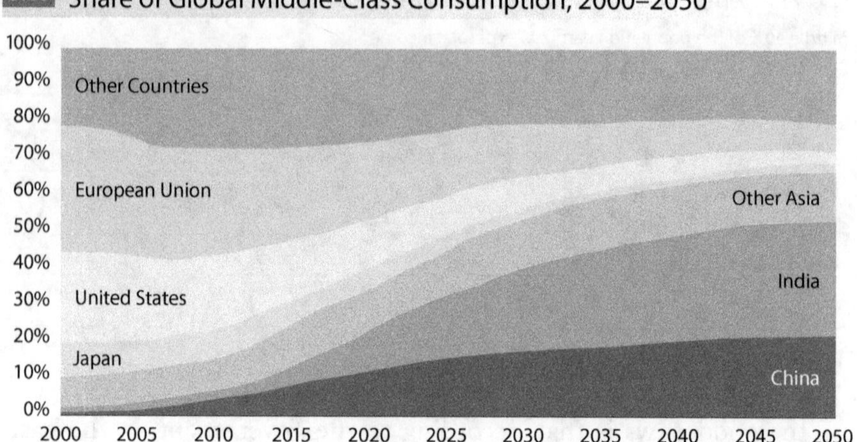

5.20 Share of Global Middle-Class Consumption, 2000–2050

Source: Kharas, H. (2010) The Emerging Middle Class in Developing Countries. OECD Development Centre, Working Paper.

Reportedly, India has a serious problem with **corruption in business and government**, but I can't document that here.

On balance, India is striving to move ahead and become part of the First World community. It could achieve that distinction within the next 50 years. All it will take is a major investment in education and software. It will happen.

As that move forward occurs, India will become a major customer for the goods of First World countries, so everybody wins.

CHAPTER 6

The European Union and Great Britain—Modestly Growing Economic Powerhouses

This chapter discusses the demographics and economy of the 27-nation European Union and United Kingdom. Despite the UK's departure from the European community, I have merged the two for purposes of discussion as they continue to trade goods and visit with one another.

6.1 European Union and United Kingdom

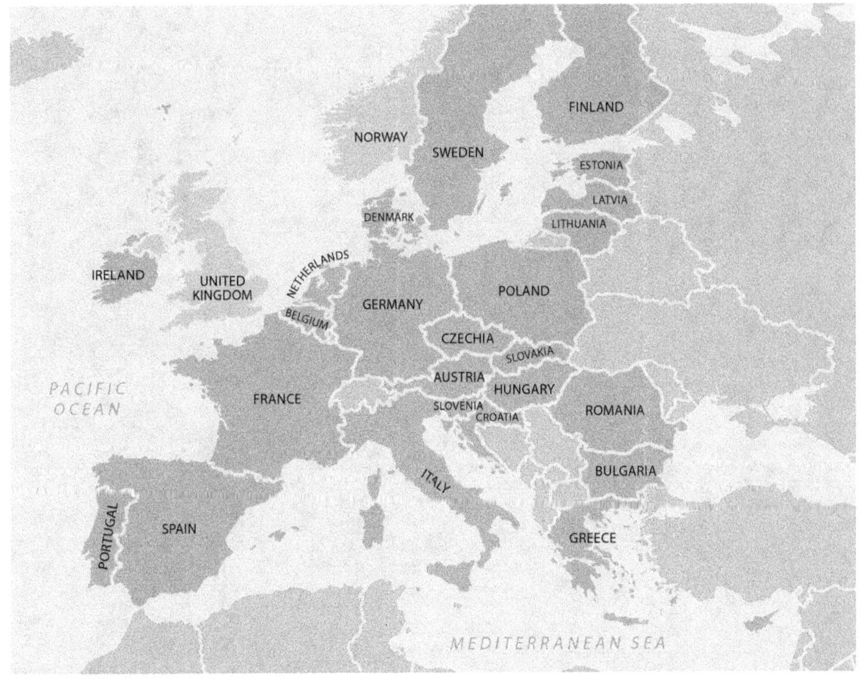

SECTION 1: DEMOGRAPHICS IN THE EUROPEAN UNION AND UNITED KINGDOM

My mantra on demographics is oft repeated: If a husband and wife do not have two kids, the economy in which they live will shrink.

And so it is with the EU/UK. Tan and brown indicate a fertility rate well below the 2.0 level:

6.2 Fertility Rate, 2019

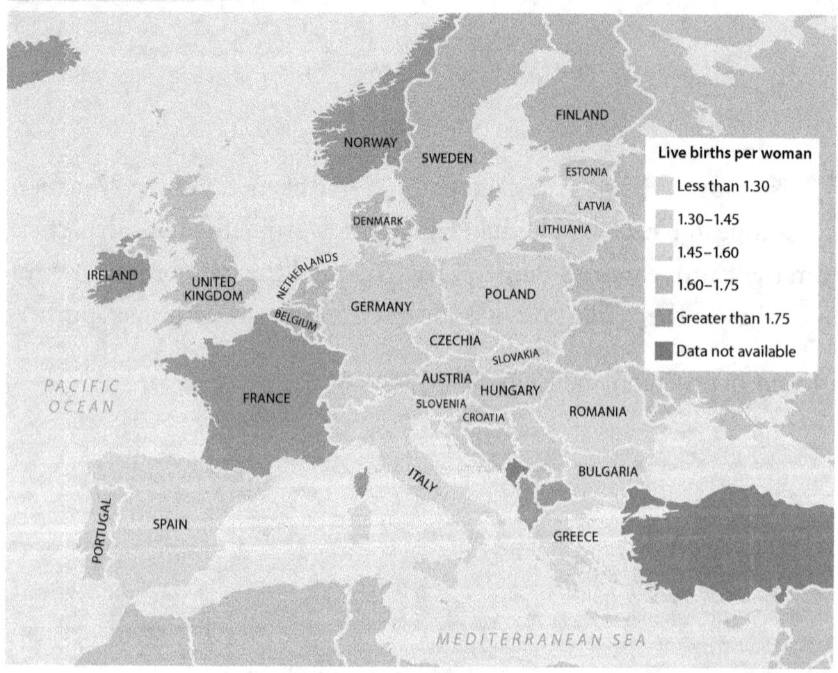

The fertility rates for five nations are shown here:

6.3 Total Fertility (Live Births Per Woman Up to Age 45)
Major Countries, 1980–2020

Country	Change 1980–2020	1980–1985	1990–1995	2005–2010	2015–2020
China	−49%	2.52	1.83	1.62	1.69
Russia	−12%	2.04	1.55	1.46	1.82
United States	−1%	1.80	2.03	2.06	1.78
European Union	**4%**	**1.62**	**1.49**	**1.64**	**1.68**
India	−117%	4.85	3.83	2.80	2.24

Source: United Nations 2020 Population Projections

As you look out to 2050, the EU/UK will have the same population that it has today, about a half billion people.

6.4 Projected Population Growth
Five Major Countries, 2020–2050

Country	2020	2050	Total	Percent
India	1,380,004,000	1,639,176,000	259,172,000	18.8%
United States	331,003,000	379,419,000	48,416,000	14.6%
EU and UK	515,557,046	515,553,621	(3,425)	−0
Russia	145,934,000	135,824,000	(10,110,000)	−6.9%
China	1,439,324,000	1,402,405,000	(36,919,000)	−2.6%

Source: United Nations Dept. of Economic and Social Affairs, Population Division

The European Union and UK and Russia suffered great losses during World War II and have seen their birthrates plummet. Russia lost 25 million people during the war.

The U.S. fertility rate has also declined, but **in-migration has saved the day**. Since 2000, the U.S. has welcomed 30 million persons to our nation, substantially more than in the past.

Unfortunately, there are no lines forming to immigrate to Russia or China.

6.5 Immigration as Percent of Population Change United States, 1940–2020

Year	Census	U.S. Change from previous decade	Percent change from Previous Decade	Legal Immigation in Decade	Legal Immigration as Percent of Population Change
1940	132,164,569	8,961,945	n/a	715,000	n/a
1950	151,325,798	19,161,229	14.5%	851,000	4%
1960	180,700,000	29,374,202	19.4%	2,494,000	8%
1970	205,100,000	24,400,000	13.5%	3,213,749	13%
1980	227,200,000	22,100,000	10.8%	4,143,000	19%
1990	249,600,000	22,400,000	9.9%	6,241,000	28%
2000	282,200,000	32,600,000	13.1%	9,769,000	30%
2010	309,300,000	27,100,000	9.6%	10,295,000	38%
2020	329,500,000	20,200,000	6.5%	10,305,000	51%

Source: U.S. Census Bureau

Of the five major nations, the European Union has the greatest decline in the percentage of the population that is under age 18:

6.6 Percent of Population Under Age 18 Major Countries, 1980–2020

Country	2020 as Percent of 1980	1980	2000	2020
India	70%	45.4%	41.1%	31.7%
United States	79%	28.1%	26.0%	22.2%
Russia	81%	26.4%	23.3%	21.4%
China	49%	42.7%	29.8%	21.1%
Europe	**71%**	**27.0%**	**21.7%**	**19.1%**

Source: United Nations 2017 Population Projections

Conversely, Europe's over-age-65 population has ballooned and now accounts for one of every five persons.

The graph below provides a vivid picture of the balance of this century. It means that the population that is now under

6.7 Percent of Population Over Age 65 Major Countries, 1980–2020

Country	1980	2000	2020
European Union	**12.4%**	**14.7%**	**19.1%**
United States	11.6%	12.3%	16.6%
Russia	10.3%	12.4%	15.5%
China	4.7%	6.8%	12.0%
India	3.6%	4.4%	6.6%

Source: United Nations 2017 Population Projections

age 18 is going to be saddled with the responsibility for taking care of the senior population.

6.8 Old Age Dependency, 2020–2100

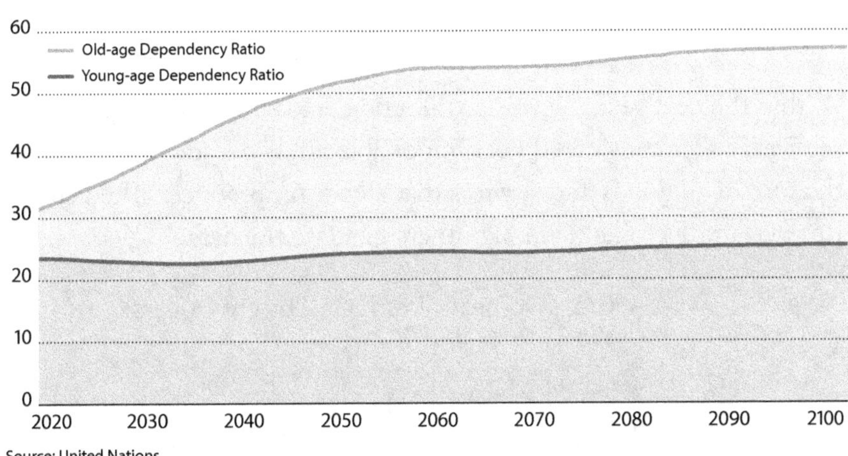

Source: United Nations

It is unlikely that this situation will change. The result of this trending is clearly shown in exhibit 6.9:

6.9 Projected Population, European Union, 2020–2100

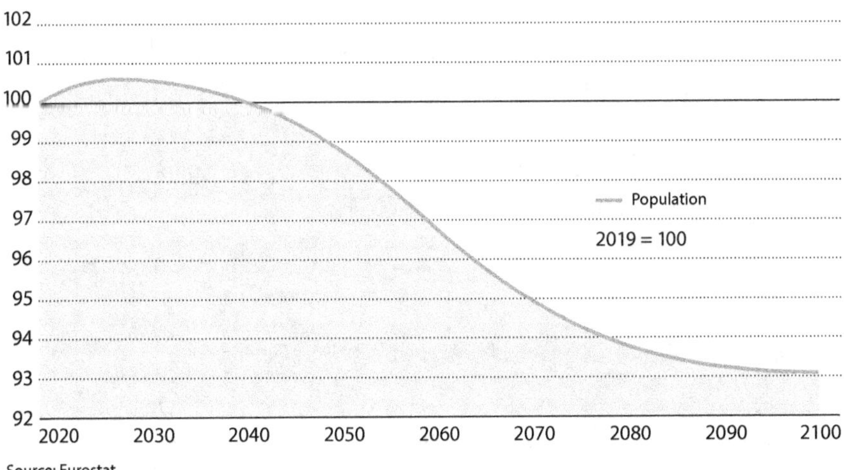

Source: Eurostat

Both Russia and China have developed government programs to increase the fertility rates. Perhaps the EU and the UK will do the same thing.

SECTION 2: THE ECONOMIC EXPANSION OF THE EU & UK

Within the next year, the world will produce $100 trillion in goods and services, a feat considered near impossible a few decades ago. GDP is the sum of all goods and services that a country produces. The Federal Reserve and Eurobank among others tabulate the data.

6.10 Gross Domestic Product[1] (Current Dollars) World, 2000 and 2021

Country	Billions	Change
1990	$22,611,431,033,122	n/a
2000	$33,607,318,755,989	$10,995,887,722,867
2010	$66,036,387,107,063	$32,429,068,351,074
2020	$87,345,300,000,000	$21,308,912,892,937
2021	$96,100,091,000,000	$8,754,791,000,000

1. Not inflation adjusted

Source: World Bank DataBank

Five nations account for almost two-thirds of that total, dominated by the big three: U.S., China, and the European Union/United Kingdom.

6.11 Gross Domestic Product (Current Dollars – Millions) Major Countries, 2000 and 2021

Country	2000	2021	Change	Percent Change
United States	$10,252	$22,996	$12,744	124%
EU and UK	$10,567	$21,086	$10,519	100%
China	$1,211	$17,734	$16,523	1364%
India	$468	$3,173	$2,705	578%
Russia	$259	$1,775	$1,516	585%
The Big 5	**$22,757**	**$66,764**	**$44,007**	**193%**

Source: World Bank DataBank and CIA Fact Book

This colorful map graphically pinpoints the nations' GDP. Dark green is the U.S., bright green is China, and the EU is a combination of colors.

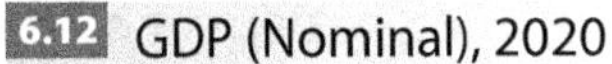

6.12 GDP (Nominal), 2020

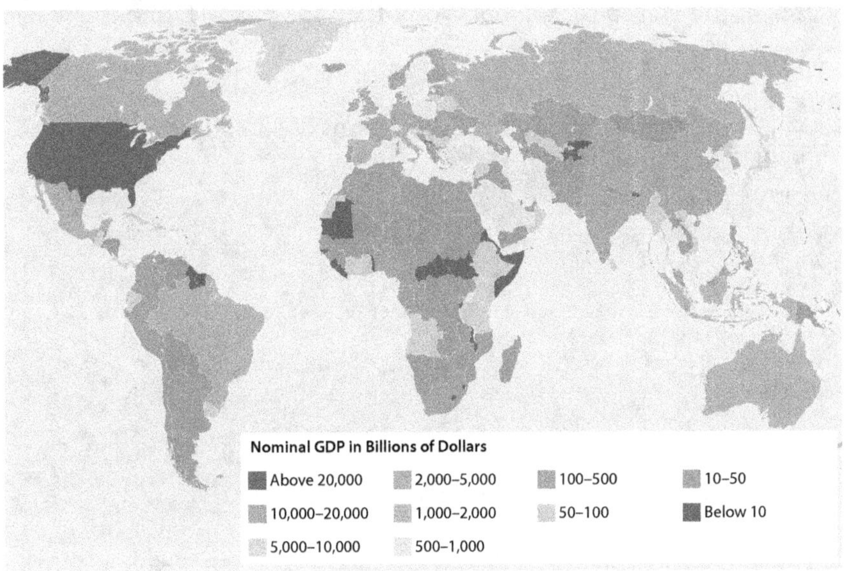

Over the years, I have found that documenting **GDP per capita** is an excellent way to determine the economic progress of a nation. Inevitably, I use the U.S. as the bellwether; it has almost doubled its GDP per capita in the past two decades.

China's gains have been incredible, as have India's. The EU and United Kingdom have gradually moved forward but have been continually hampered by demographics.

6.13 GDP Per Capita[1]
Major Countries, 2000 and 2021

Country	2000	2021	Change 2000/2021	Percent Change
United States	$36,334	$69,287	$32,953	90.7%
EU and UK	$27,987	$44,500	$16,513	59.0%
Russia	$1,771	$12,172	$10,401	587.3%
China	$959	$12,556	$11,597	1209.3%
India	$443	$2,277	$1,834	414.0%

1. 2018 GDP converted into U.S. Dollars divided into the avg. Population

Source: International Monetary Fund

Exhibit 6.14 displays business registrations and declarations of bankruptcy in the European Union. Other than the COVID months, their economy has been stable.

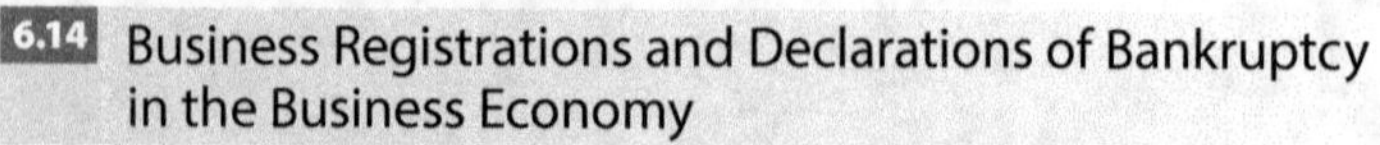

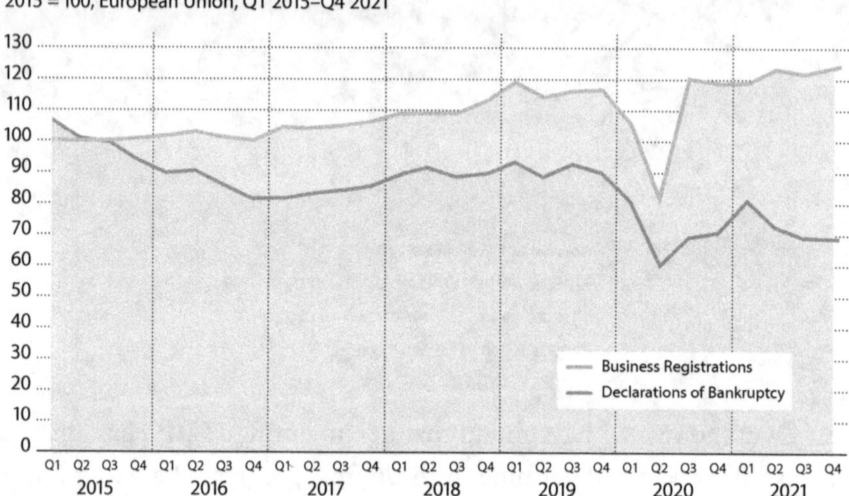

SECTION 3: THE ECONOMY OF EUROPE
AND THE UK AS STAND-ALONES

In this section, I have looked at the United Kingdom and the European Union, which were joined together until January 1, 2021.

The **United Kingdom** is composed of England, Wales, Scotland, and Northern Ireland. The European Union includes 27 countries.

It appears that neither has greatly suffered from the split-up, although both are now guided by an arcane trade agreement. It is too early to tell if there will be a major economic effect on the UK, although many are predicting doomsday. The UK has remained a ratio of 17% of the EU employment.

6.15 Employment
European Union and United Kingdom, 2016–2021

Year	United Kingdom		European Union		UK as a Percent of EU
	Millions	Index	Millions	Index	
2015	31,540	1.00	186,889	1.00	17%
2016	31,845	1.01	189,335	1.01	17%
2017	32,154	1.02	191,991	1.03	17%
2018	32,597	1.03	193,745	1.04	17%
2019	32,934	1.04	195,796	1.05	17%
2020[1]	32,159	1.02	192,862	1.03	17%
2021	32,667	1.04	195,172	1.04	17%

1. COVID March 2020

Source: United Nations

Both are recovering from COVID:

6.16 Gross Domestic Product (dollars)
United Kingdom[1]

Year	United Kingdom		European Union		UK as a Percent of EU
	Billions	Index	Billions	Index	
2015	$2.953	1.00	13.55	1.00	22%
2016	$2.693	0.91	13.89	1.03	19%
2017	$2.662	0.90	14.77	1.09	18%
2018	$2.857	0.97	15.98	1.18	18%
2019	$2.831	0.96	15.69	1.16	18%
2020	$2.781	0.94	15.30	1.13	18%
2021	$2.830	0.96	17.09	1.26	17%

1. England, Wales, Scotland, Northern Ireland

Source: International Monetary Fund

COVID ruined the tourism industry for the past three years, but it is gradually coming back.

6.17 Tourism (Inbound Visits), United Kingdom

Year	Millions Pounds	Index
2017	$28,400,000	n/a
2018	$26,500,000	0.93
2019	$28,500,000	1.00
2020	$6,200,000	0.22
2021	$7,400,000	0.26
2022[1]	$16,900,000	0.60

1. Projected

Source: British Tourism Authority

The 2021-22 figures are not yet available because it has proven difficult to get 27 countries coordinated.

Factory orders have recovered in the UK and the EU, as these graphs show:

6.18 Tourism (Inbound Visits) European Union		
Year	In Dollars	Index
2016	$1,373,256,963	
2017	$1,426,568,889	$1.04
2018	$1,514,835,659	1.10
2019	$1,514,835,659	1.10
2020	$1,009,388,581	0.74
2021	n\a	

Source: Eurostat

6.19 Factory Orders, United Kingdom, 2014–2020

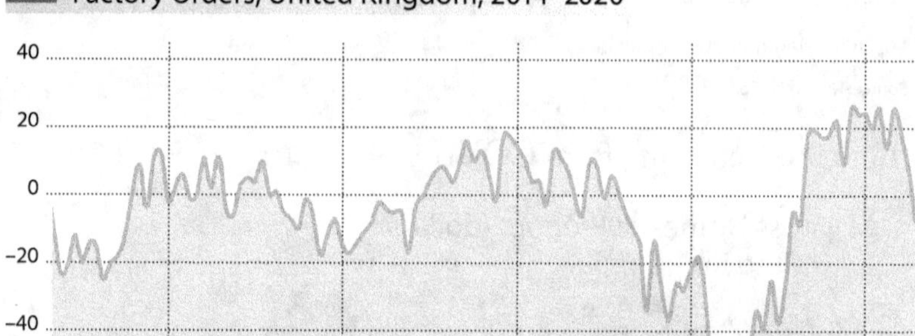

Source: Eurostat

6.20 Evolution of European Union's Value of Sold Industrial Production, 2011–2021

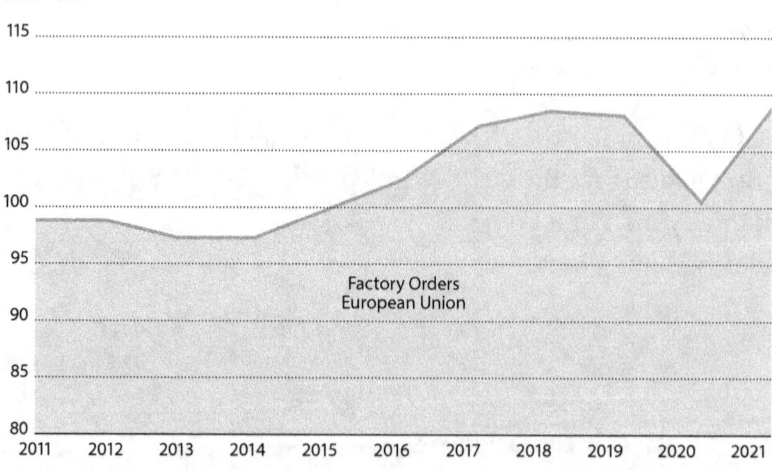

Source: Eurostat

The Little Countries

Europe has a broad array of small countries. Among them are Lithuania, Latvia, Estonia, and Finland.

All have benefitted from out-migration from Russia over the past two decades. Having visited these countries (shortly before COVID), I was impressed by the architecture, cleanliness, friendliness, and the fact that almost everyone spoke English.

A wonderful example of a "small country" is Estonia, with 1.3 million people. It is pioneering an e-government initiative that allows Estonians to go online to vote, pay taxes, and appear in court, all with a "digital identity card."

Estonia is proving to be a giant in the digital era. It is the home of the founders of Skype and other technology startups.

Office Vacancy Rates

One last indicator of **economic health** is office vacancy rates. Both Paris and London have acceptable vacancy rates, far lower than New York or Los Angeles.

6.21 Office Vacancy Rates
London, New York City, Paris, and Los Angeles, 2020–2022

Year	Paris CBD	London CBD	NY	LA
2019	2.1%	5.7%	7.9%	90.7%
2020	4.2%	4.2%	8.9%	192.0%
2nd Qtr 2021	4.5%	7.9%	10.9%	15.4%
1st Qtr. 2022	3.5%	7.9%	16.9%	13.1%
1st Qtr. 2023	7.9%	8.6%	22.2%	27.9%

Source: Cushman Wakefield; Colliers

The long and the short of it is that Brexit hasn't been a disaster, although it shouldn't have happened to begin with. It will continue to mean an enormous amount of paperwork for those involved in business trading, but that will produce more jobs.

Overall, both the EU and the UK will do just fine. All they need is more kids and more time.

SECTION 4: HOME OWNERSHIP IN THE EU

The stability of modern Europe is tied, in part, to its high rate of home ownership. Several of the countries have ownership rates in excess of 80%. The U.S. is 67%.

6.22 Home Ownership, Selected Countries, European Union

Country	Percent Own with No Mortgage	Percent Own	Total O–O
Netherlands	8.4%	60.7%	69.1%
Sweden	12.3%	52.1%	64.4%
Germany	19.0%	31.5%	50.5%
France	33.5%	30.5%	64.0%
Portugal	38.4%	38.9%	77.3%
Spain	44.8%	30.3%	75.1%
Turkey	46.9%	8.0%	57.9%
Italy	59.9%	15.2%	75.1%
Poland	72.5%	13.1%	85.6%
Lithuania	74.5%	14.0%	88.5%

Source: Eurostat

As a final note on the EU and UK, with its population shrinking, there will be fewer household formations and, as a result, there will be a continual decline in demand for housing and household goods and vehicles. It will be a very slow decline, but a decline nonetheless.

The one important caveat: It is entirely possible that **out-migration** from Russia and other downtrodden countries to the EU and UK may be so severe that it will cause the present diminishing projections to reverse the downward trend.

CHAPTER 7

California
The Land of the Free, Home of the Ingenious

California is a state, but it's also like a country, and, by any measure, it is a state of mind.

It doesn't have a king or a president, but other than that, California can do most everything a country can do except print money. But, of course, it can spend money, and unlike a real nation it cannot operate in the "red."

Folks regularly talk about people leaving California because of its high cost of living. There is more to it than that.

First, the **birthrate** in California has declined steadily for the past 60 years (births per 1,000 population).

7.1 Comparative Population California and Like-Size Nations

Spain	46,755,000
California	**39,542,000**
Poland	37,847,000
Canada	37,742,000
Australia	25,500,000

7.2 Births and Deaths, California, 1960–2021

July, Year	Births		Deaths		Births Minus Deaths
	Births	Crude Birth Rate	Deaths	Crude Death Rate	
1960	372,000	23.5	135,000	8.5	237,000
1980	390,000	16.4	180,000	7.6	210,000
2000	525,000	15.4	228,000	6.7	297,000
2021	420,000	10.7	344,000	8.7	76,000

Source: CA Department of Demographics

Second, **in-migration** has slowed down, particularly due to COVID and the Trump anti-migration mandates in the past few years.

That said, in the past 20 years, the state has gained five and a half million people. That is more people than live in Oregon, Utah, or Nevada.

7.3 Migration California, 1960–2021

"July, Year"	Number	Crude Migration Rate[1]
1960	338,000	21.3
1980	315,000	13.2
2000	285,000	8.4
2021	–249,000	–6.3

1. per 1,000 population

Source: CA Dept. of Demographics

7.4 Picture: Changing Population Trends California, 1960–2021

"July, Year"	Population	Number[1]	Percent	Natural Increase (births minus deaths)	Migration
1960	15,863,000	575,000	3.76%	237,000	338
1980	23,782,000	525,000	2.26%	210,000	315
2000	34,001,000	582,000	1.74%	297,000	285
2021	39,369,000	–173,000	0.03%	76,000	–249
2000–2021	5,368,000				

1. Natural increase plus migration

Optimally, with COVID on the wane, the birth and death rate will return to normalcy. But I suspect that the foreign in-migration will not return to historic norms and it is highly likely that net domestic out-migration will continue unabated.

SECTION 1: THE DEPENDABLY CHANGING DEMOGRAPHY OF CALIFORNIA

Based on recent birthrates, the California Department of Finance has projected the population changes in California over the next 40 years.

In the 2020-2060 timeframe, the state is expected to add 4.0+ million population. The not-so-good news is that virtually all that gain is folks over 60 years of age.

That does not augur well for growth of the California economy. Seniors just don't spend as much as younger people, except for healthcare. Healthcare is important, but it does not generate the dollars that younger households spend. But geriatric care is definitely a growth industry.

7.5 Population Projection by Age Group California, 2020–2060

Age Group	2020	2060	Change 2020–2060	Percent
1 to 19	10,107,492	9,019,162	(1,088,330)	–11%
20 to 39	10,803,172	10,366,964	(436,208)	–4%
40 to 59	10,104,684	10,607,087	502,403	5%
60 to 79	7,363,295	9,222,638	1,859,343	25%
80+	1,516,788	5,010,885	3,494,097	230%
Total	39,895,431	44,226,736	4,331,305	11%
1 to 39	20,910,664	19,386,126	(1,524,538)	(0)
60+	8,880,083	14,233,523	5,353,440	60%

Source: CA Department of Demographics

The projections in Exhibit 7.6 give rise to projections of **K-12 enrollment**. During the next 10 years, **the state projects that K-12 enrollment will decline by more than a half million students.**

In a similar mode, the number of high school graduates in the next decade will decline by more than 50,000, or 12.6%.

School economics: there will be a substantial number of K-12 schools shuttered and a substantial decline in community college and four-year college enrollment. It also means that

7.6 Projected K-12 Enrollment California, 2021–2032

Year	Enrollment
2021–2022	5,892,240
2031–2032	5,368,555
Change	(523,685)
Percent Changed	–8.9%

Source: Ca. Dept. of Finance

7.7 High School Graduates California, 2020–2032

Year	Number
2020–2031	433,740
2031–2032	379,299
Change	(54,441)
Percent Changed	–12.6%

Source: Ca. Dept. of Finance

federal funds will decline and instead go to those more youthful states with growing enrollments.

Obviously, a move to increase foreign in-migration of younger adults could reverse the trend.

SECTION 2: TAXATION AND ECONOMIC GROWTH

There is a strong correlation between taxation and economic growth. In the following exhibit, we show the population change in the past 20 years and the income tax in several states. Pointedly, the states with the lowest or no personal tax have had the highest rates of population gain.

Notably, California is the land of the "not so free."

7.8 Tax Comparison and Rate of Growth California and Selected States (1)

State	Population Change Percent 2000–2020	Income Tax	Flat Tax	Graduated Tax	Top Percent Tax
California	16%			Yes	13.3%
New York	6%			Yes	10.9%
Georgia	31%			Yes	5.8%
Arizona	40%			Yes	4.5%
Nevada	56%	No			
Texas	40%	No			
Florida	35%	No			
Washington	31%	No			
North Carolina	27%		Yes		

1. 4Q2020–4Q2021

7.9 Top Marginal Rates, State Taxes

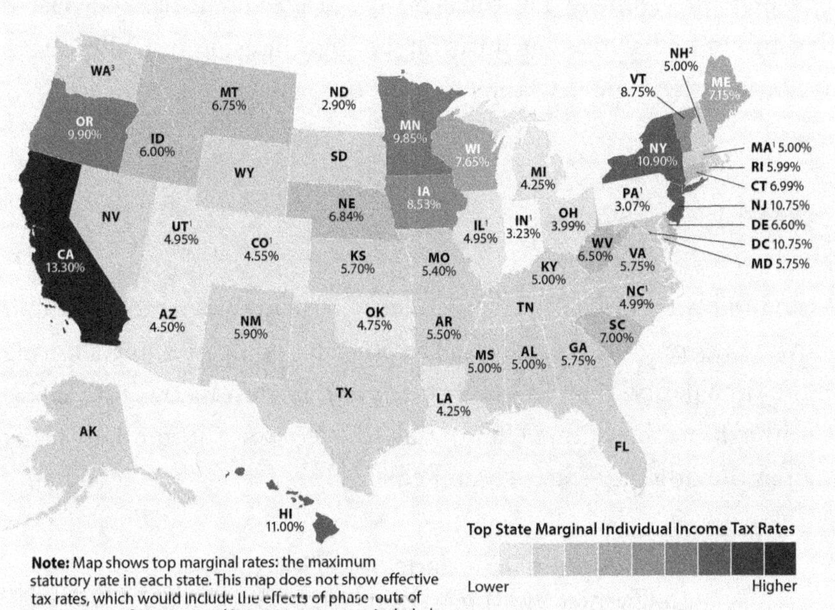

Note: Map shows top marginal rates: the maximum statutory rate in each state. This map does not show effective tax rates, which would include the effects of phase outs of various tax preferences. Local income taxes are not included. Missouri's top marginal rate will be reduced to 5.3% if certain revenue triggers are met.

1. State has a flat income tax.

2. State only taxes interest and dividends income.

3. State only taxes capital gains income.

Source: Tax Foundation

It is certainly true that the other states with low income tax make up for it with higher property tax rates and, in some cases, higher sales tax rates. Note the property taxes in those states with no income tax.

7.10 Tax Comparison California and Other Fast-Growing States

State	Percent Population Gain 2000–2020	Effectuve Property Tax Rate	Sales Tax	Income Tax	Flat Tax	Graduated Tax	Top Percent
California	15.8%	0.76%	8.8%			Yes	13.3%
New York	6.2%	1.72%	8.5%			Yes	10.9%
Georgia	31.0%	0.92%	7.4%			Yes	5.8%
Arizona	39.9%	0.66%	8.5%			Yes	4.5%
North Carolina	27.3%	0.98%	7.0%		Yes		
Washington	31.0%	0.98%	9.3%	No			
Texas	40.1%	1.75%	8.2%	No			
Florida	35.0%	0.89%	7.0%	No			
Nevada	55.8%	0.60%	8.2%	No			

Of major importance to Californians, property taxes can only be increased 2.0% annually, regardless of how much a home has appreciated. That has to be balanced against the fact that housing in California is obviously more expensive than in most other states.

California Tax Revenue

As an indication of California's resilience, we have prepared an exhibit showing tax revenue collected in the 50 states compared to California in the time period that COVID struck to the latest figures (2Q 2022).

The exhibit shows that California's recovery was substantially faster than in the other 49 states combined:

7.11 Tax Revenue (Hundeds of Millions)
California and the Nation, 2020Q1–2Q2022

Year	Qtr.	50 States	Index		California	Indexes
2020	1	317,869	83.3%		56,477	1.0%
2020[1]	2	293,381	92.3%		48,208	85.4%
2020	3	306,468	96.4%		54,031	95.7%
2020	4	309,724	97.4%		55.610	99.3%
2021	1	314,906	99.1%		58,148	103.0%
2021	2	352,680	111.0%		70,476	124.8%
2021	3	347,988	109.5%		66,505	117.8%
2021	4	360,982	113.6%		69,294	122.7%
2022	1	374,041	117.7%		73,904	130.9%
2022	2	381,666	120.1%		74,221	141.4%

1. COVID strikes

Source: California Dept. of Financa

7.12 Tax Collected (Inflation Adjusted)
United States, Q1 2020 to Q2 2022

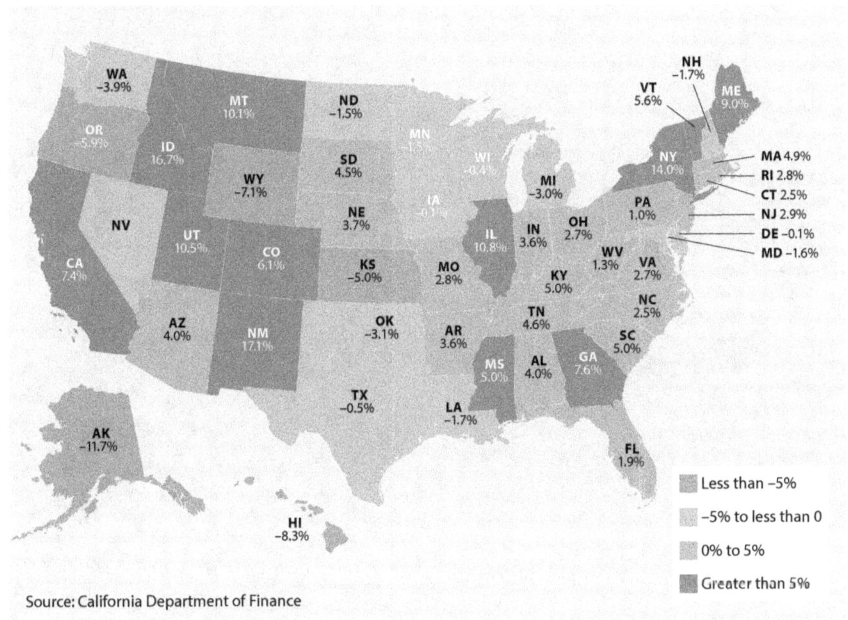

Source: California Department of Finance

SECTION 3: POPULATION WAVE

Make no mistake about it: the population of the nation is moving west. The Census Bureau has been tracking population movement for decades. The path of movement is now about halfway across the country. The path tends to follow the jobs.

The population is working its way toward **Texas**, Arizona, and Nevada, but not in the direction of California.

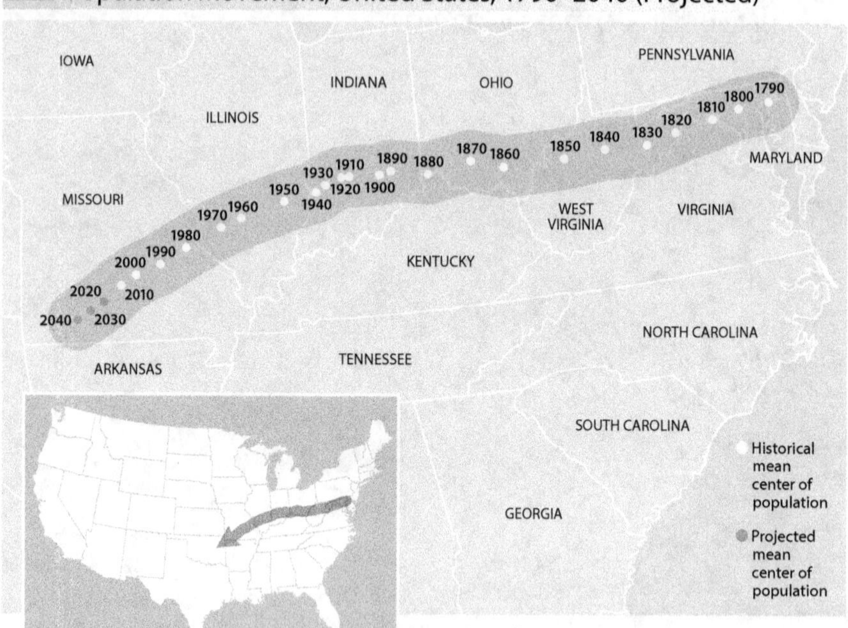

Source: Census Bureau

California Ethnicity

In the past 40 years, there has been a major ethnicity shift in California. In that 40-year period, virtually all of the increase in population has been Hispanic and Asian. The non-Hispanic white population has declined by 10% in that 40-year period.

The Hispanic population is predominantly of Mexican heritage but there is a substantial influx from Central America.

7.14 Changing Ethnicity
California, 1980-2020

Ethnicity	1980		2020		Change	Percent Change
Non-Hispanice White	15,950,120	67%	14,365,145	37%	(1,584,975)	–10%
Hispanic	4,615,711	19%	15,380,929	39%	10,765,218	69%
Asian	1,257,408	5%	5,743,983	15%	4,486,575	29%
Black	1,794,051	8%	2,142,371	5%	348,320	2%
Other	164,710	1%	1,731,595	4%	1,566,885	10%
Total	23,782,000	100%	39,346,023	100%	15,564,023	100%
Total Hispanic and Asian	5,873,119		21,124,912		15,251,793	
Percent of Total		25%		54%		**98%**

Source: U.S. Census

Educational Attainment

Importantly, California has maintained equilibrium with the nation in terms of educational attainment.

7.15 Percent of Persons Over Age 25
Educational Attainment, U.S. and California, 2020

Degree	U.S.	California
Bachelor's Degree	23.5%	22.1%
Advanced Degree	14.3%	14.0%
Total	37.8%	36.1%

Source: U.S. Census

A final thought on education: The state has a desperate need for experienced labor. Much of that need can be satisfied with persons who have great experience but do not have a four-year college degree. Degrees are great, but they are not everything.

SECTION 4: THE BUSINESS OF CALIFORNIA

Gross domestic product (GDP) is the total sum of goods and services produced by a country. In the 50 years we have been tracking the world's growth, it is somewhat remarkable that the GDP has increased more than seven times and it is closing in on $100 trillion.

In 1950, the U.S. GDP was $1.0 trillion. In 2020, it had **expanded 20-fold** and now accounts for one quarter of the world's GDP.

Of equal interest, the state of California has the fifth largest GDP in the world and is fast approaching the output of Germany.

7.16 Gross Domestic Product (Trillion of Dollars)
Major Countries, A 50-Year Pictrure, 1970–2020

Country	1970	Percent of World	2020	Percent of World
World	**$12.14**		**$87.70**	
United States	$1.07	8.84%	$21.43	24.44%
China	$0.09	0.76%	$14.34	16.35%
Japan	$0.21	1.70%	$5.08	5.79%
Germany	$0.20	1.67%	$3.86	4.40%
California	**$0.11**	**0.91%**	**$3.30**	**3.76%**
India	$0.06	0.51%	$2.87	3.27%
United Kingdom	$0.12	1.01%	$2.83	3.23%
Russia	$0.21	1.70%	$1.70	1.94%
South Korea	$0.08	0.66%	$1.65	1.88%
Mexico	$0.04	0.32%	$1.27	1.45%

Sources: World Bank, Directorate of Intelligence, CIA

In Exhibit 7.17 we show the change in the California GDP over the past 40 years. It shows that in recessionary periods, **the GDP grows by 2.0-3.0% and in good times by 7.0-8.0%.**

7.17 California State Gross Domestic Product (GDP)
(Millions of Dollars)

Year	Event	Current Dollars	1997 Dollars	Deflator 1997=100	Current Dollars	Annual Percent Change 1997 Dollars	Deflator
1980	Recession	327,959	599,507	54.7	11.7%	3.0%	8.5%
1990		773,460	906,103	85.4	7.0%	2.9%	3.9%
2000		1,356,975	1,696,172	80.0	9.3%	7.7%	1.4%
2010	Recession	1,954,093	2,036,015	96.0	3.4%	2.0%	1.3%
2020	COVID	3,007,188	2,663,666	112.9	-1.5%	-2.8%	1.3%
2021		3,373,240	2,871,424	116.9	11.6%	7.8%	3.5%

Last updated: May, 2022 – New 2021, Revised 1997 onwards.

The next release of GDP by state is scheduled for September 2022.

Sources: US Bureau of Economic Analysis

We have divided the U.S. into three sections, all of which are high-growth regions: West Coast, Texas, and the Southeast. **The eight states in these three regions account for 40% of the nation's GDP.**

7.18 Gross Domestic Product (GDP)
United States and Selected States, 2000–2021

2021 Ranking (High to Low)	Millions	
	2000	2021
United States	$10,250,952	$22,996,086
The West Coast		
California	$1,192,245	$3,356,631
Oregon	$111,715	$266,943
Washington	$237,378	$667,576
Total	$1,541,338	$4,291,150
Percent of the Nation	15%	19%
Texas		
Texas	$738,677	$1,985,319
Percent of the Nation	7%	9%
The Great Southeast		
North Carolina	$278,008	$654,985
South Carolina	$115,320	$270,079
Georgia	$305,572	$683,302
Florida	$490,429	$1,226,298
Washington	$237,378	$667,576
Total	$1,189,329	$2,834,664
Percent of the Nation	12%	12%
3 Regional Areas as Percent of U.S	34%	40%

Source: U.S. Bureau of Economic Analysis

SECTION 5: CALIFORNIA'S REVENUES

With the exception of the 2020 COVID interruption, the California economy has moved forward on a bullish basis. **Personal Income** is the prime source of operating funds for California, accounting for three-fourths of total revenues. This revenue source has virtually doubled since 2015, and without COVID, would have been even further ahead.

7.19 General Fund Revenues (Millions), California, 2015–2021

Year	Personal Income	Sales and Use	Corporation
2015	$24,192	$10,191	$970
2016	$25,953	$10,379	$1,448
2017	$27,538	$10,247	$1,794
2018	$30,711	$10,948	$2,103
2019	$31,472	$11,193	$2,690
2020	$52,537	$11,721	$7,694
2021	$45,220	$12,755	$5,181
Change 2015–2021	21,028	2,564	4,211
Percent Change	87%	25%	434%
Annual Percent Change	12%	4%	62%

Source: CA Dept of Finance

Business Formations

Another strong indicator of economic growth is business formations. California is **one of the big three** in business formations:

7.20 Business Formations by State, CY, 2021

State	Rank	Number
Florida	1	632,105
California	2	518,001
Texas	3	492,243
Georgia	4	326,460
New York	5	309,170

Source: Census

Employment by Category and Metropolitan Area

Over the past several years, California has had a substantial gain in jobs. Despite the COVID years, the state has continued to gain jobs in virtually every category. Most importantly, there has been very positive growth in the professional and business services category, traditionally the best paying category. It is also the category that includes jobs in the sciences and software and other growth industries.

7.21 Change in Employment
Selected Categories California, 2015–2022

Category	2015	2022	Change	Percent Change
Construction	761,000	923,000	162,000	21.3%
Education and Health Services	2,505,000	2,928,000	423,000	16.9%
Professional and Business Services	2,540,000	2,847,000	307,000	12.1%
Trade Transportation and Utilities	2,929,000	3,157,000	228,000	7.8%
Leisure and Hospitality	1,866,500	1,905,000	38,500	2.1%
Government	2,483,000	2,531,000	48,000	1.9%
Manufacturing	1,307,000	1,311,000	4,000	0.3%

Source: BLS

Within California, the strongest growth in employment has been in Northern California, thanks to massive expansion of the software industries. There does appear to be some slowdown in that sector of the professions, but not dramatic.

7.22 Employment by Metropolitan Area California, 2015–2022

Area	2015	2022	Change	Percent Change
Bay Area	2,310,000	2,466,000	156,000	6.8%
Sacramento	940,000	1,050,000	110,000	11.7%
SanDiego	1,416,000	1,509,000	93,000	6.6%
Santa Clara County	1,071,000	1,164,000	93,000	8.7%
Los Angeles	4,399,000	4,491,000	92,000	2.1%
Orange County	1,584,000	1,664,000	80,000	5.1%

Source: BLS

Exports

79% of California's top 10 exports are high-tech:

7.23 Top Ten Exports Goods (In Millions) California, 2021

1	High-Tech	Electrical Machinery	$26,928
2	High-Tech	Industrial Machinery	$25,039
3	High-Tech	Precision Instruments	$15,973
4	High-Tech	Motor Vehicles and Parts	$11,085
6	High-Tech	Aircraft	$6,608
8	High-Tech	Pharmaceuticals	$4,578
5		Fruit and Nuts	$10,492
7		Precious Stones andl Metals	$5,632
9		Plastics	$4,165
10		Chemicals	$3,836
Total – Top Ten			$114,336
High-Tech			$90,211
High-Tech			78.9%

Source: California Department of Finance

Venture Capital

Venture capital is the lifeblood of the life sciences and software industries. And California has taken the lead in attracting venture capital.

7.24 California Venture Capital Funding (In Billions of Dollars)

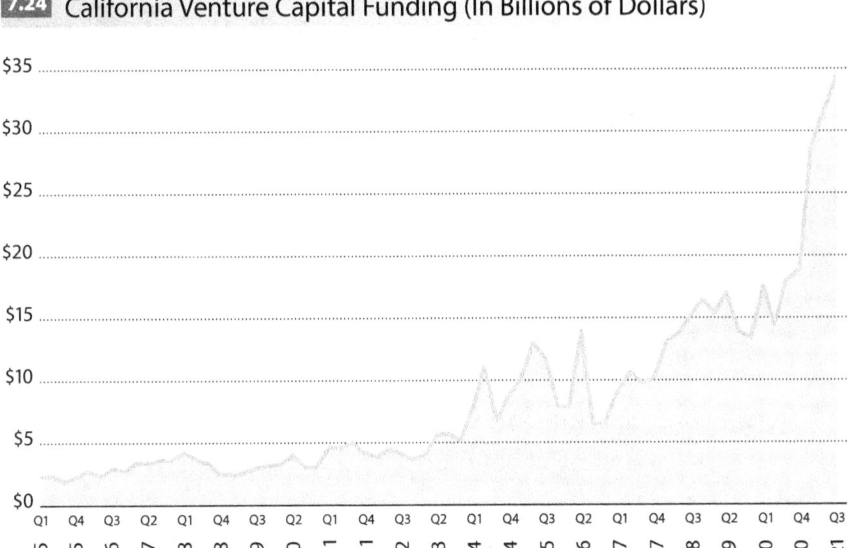

For the past decade, California has attracted more than 40% of the venture capital in the U.S., **almost three times the number two state.**

7.25 Venture Capital History ($Millions) Top Five States, 2012–2022

State	2012	2017	2022	2012–2017	2017–2022
California	$19,427	$42,538	$104,427	$23,111	$61,889
Massachusetts	$4,509	$9,827	$21,121	$5,318	$11,294
New York	$2,757	$12,007	$28,987	$9,250	$16,980
Texas	$2,258	$3,045	$9,548	$787	$6,503
Washington	$1,447	$2,144	$8,090	$697	$5,946
United States	**$41,700**	**$90,100**	**$238,300**	**$48,400**	**$148,200**
California as Percent of U.S.	**47%**	**47%**	**44%**	**48%**	**42%**

Source: Pitchbook

In summary, California is an amazing economic machine and has been for decades; however, this decade and those that follow will see leveling out of the machine as a result of a slowly declining population.

The declining population is a direct result of the **paucity of reasonably priced sale and rental housing**—a situation that can be fixed by government, but unfortunately will not be. It's a shame but the folks we elect to represent us in California just don't seem to care. Or maybe they don't understand the problem.

The answer to the problem is really twofold: (1) fixing the housing problem and (2) fostering immigration from both the U.S. and other nations.

Dream on.

SECTION 6: HOUSING CALIFORNIANS

If as much effort was put forth in the development of housing as has been put forth in writing about the need for it, there would be a balance of supply and demand.

When Governor Newsome campaigned for office, he stated that he would add 3.5 million homes in California. He has missed by 90%, but he means well.

In 2022, 107,565 units were permitted, approximately in the same proportion as the population; i.e., almost 90% was produced in urban areas:

7.26 Residential Units Permitted California, 1921–2022

Years	SFD	MF	Total
1980–1989	113,000	93,000	206,000
1990–1999	82,400	27,100	109,500
2000–2009	94,700	38,800	133,500
2010–2019	44,000	45,700	89,700
2020–2021	62,466	50,250	112,716
2021–2022	63,717	55,950	119,667

Source: U.S. Census

7.27 Residential Units Permitted
Major Metropolitan Areas, California, 2022

Area	Total	Single Family	Multi-Family	Percent MF
Northern California				
Napa	1,094	220	874	80%
Ventura County	1,326	516	810	61%
Sacramento	10,714	8,132	2,582	24%
Santa Rosa	2,265	955	1,310	58%
San Francisco-Oakland	11,048	3,248	7,800	71%
San Jose	6,783	3,694	3,089	46%
Total	**33,230**	**16,765**	**16,465**	**50%**
Central California				
Fresno	3,678	2,896	782	21%
Stockton	3,803	3,140	663	17%
Bakersfield	2,792	2,486	306	11%
Modesto	690	642	48	7%
Visalia	2,385	1,420	965	40%
Total	**13,348**	**10,584**	**2,764**	**21%**
Southern California				
Los Angeles/Orange Co.	32,593	10,996	21,597	66%
Riverside-San Bernardino	16,320	12,199	4,121	25%
San Diego	9,443	3,520	5,923	63%
Ventura	1,326	516	810	61%
Santa Barbara	1,305	441	864	66%
Total	**60,987**	**27,672**	**33,315**	**55%**
Total	**107,565**	**55,021**	**52,544**	**49%**
Percent by Region				
Northern	31%	30%	31%	66%
Central	12%	19%	5%	25%
Southern	57%	50%	63%	63%

Source: U.S. Census

There are two things that are preventing the governor from fulfilling his promise to the people:

- A paucity of zoning for multi-family housing in urban areas
- The costs of constructing higher-density housing

It is my contention that in the urban cores and those areas that are proximate to employment centers of our coastal cities, virtually 100% of new housing should be multi-family: a combination of townhomes and vertical construction.

This exhibit displays the number of units per acre for various types of multi-family housing, ranging from 10-25 units per acre to high-rises at 300-400 per acre. Notably, there is a major leap in construction costs as the structures get higher.

**7.28 Density Calculations
Residential Housing Urban Areas**

Building Type	Levels	Units Per Acre	Construction Cost/Sq.Ft.[1]
Townhomes	2–3	10–25	$120–130
Wood Frame Garden Apartments	3–4	40–50	$130–150
Mid rise	6–8	75–100	$175–200
High Rise	10+	300–400	$300–440

1. West Coast per net sq.ft

Translating those densities into what the units would rent or sell for is shown in 7.29 below. These rents and costs relate to urban areas in California.

**7.29 Rent and Sale Price Calculations
New Market-Rate Residential Housing
Urban Areas, California**

Building Type	Unit Sq.Ft.	Rent/Month if apts.	Sale Price as Condominiums
Townhomes	1,000–2,000	$3,000–4,500	$700,000–1,000,000
Wood Frame Garden Apartments	700–1,200	$2,500–3,500	$500,000–700,000
Mid-rise	700–1,200	$3,000–3,500	$600,000–800,000
High-Rise	700–1,200	$3,000–5,000	$800,000–1,000,000+

The incomes required to provide a market for these products is equally steep. Typically, rental projects require a 2.5-3.0 ratio of income to rent. Therefore, a $3,000/month apartment would require a $7,500-9,000 per month income. For a "for sale" home, with a 20% down payment, there would be a need for a $168,000 household income. Very steep!

7.30 Income Required to Quality Rental or Sale Housing, Urban Areas, California

Rental Apartments	
Typical Rent Per Month	$3,000
Annualized	$36,000
Income to Rent Ratio:	2.5–3.0
Annual Income Required	$90,000–108,000

Sale Housing	
Average Price	$700,000
Loan Percent	80%
Loan Amount	$560,000
Annual Income Required Percent	30%
Annual Income Required	$168,000

The steep apartment rent and prices relate to three factors:

1. the high price of land

2. the high price of labor

3. government fees

I do not anticipate that any of the three will be reduced in the foreseeable future.

There are two ways that can be utilized to bring down the cost of housing:

First, **the subsidization of rents** (i.e., affordable housing)—a type of housing production that is generated by the use of tax credits and other financial mechanisms. "Affordable housing" is typically available only for rental housing.

Second, **ground leases** on government-owned land (civilian or military). Most municipalities have a generous supply of city-owned vacant land that could be leased to developers, either for rental or sale housing. Typically, the city would recapture the land value at some point when the project or homes are ultimately sold. The city would also delay the payment of fees. In most cities in urban areas, the fees per unit are in the $30,000-50,000 per unit range, and sometimes higher.

Overall, it is folly to believe that the price of housing in California will be reduced. And the percent of housing to be produced as "affordable" or on ground leases will continue to be minimal.

Therefore, it is logical to assume that the paucity of housing that will be built in the urban areas will continue and, as a result, the population growth of California will be minimal if not negligible in the coming decades.

But, also remember that a state with almost 40 million population and plentiful jobs will continue to be an economic powerhouse for many decades. California is a very likable economic and climatic environment with an exceptional number of jobs that pay very well.

Over the years, the number of labor-intensive jobs that are now available will be mechanized and therefore reduce the long-term demand for blue-collar labor. It's just a matter of time.

And we do not know yet the effect of the "work at home" phenomenon. Because humans crave interaction, workers are gradually returning to the office.

SECTION 7: FINAL THOUGHTS ON CALIFORNIA

The Fraser Institute has been keeping track of what they call **Economic Freedom** for many years. Their last report was 2018. In that report, they rate states on their economic freedom based on **property rights, labor market freedom, taxes, and government spending.**

Of the big three, Florida comes in No. 2 in the nation; Texas No. 4, and **California, a rousing No. 47.** What are Californians doing wrong?

7.31 Economic Freedom, United States, 2018

State	Score	Rank
Florida	7.73	2
Texas	7.61	4
California	4.71	47

Source: Fraser Institute

Fortune 1,000

There are 118 Fortune 1,000 firms headquartered in California. There were more but in the 2018-2021 period, 11 headquarters move out of state, half of them to Texas. That doesn't mean that they moved all their employees, but moving the headquarters makes a statement that California isn't as attractive to business as it once was.

7.32 Fortune 1,000 Headquarters that Left California, 2018–2021

Company	Destination	Fortune Ranking
McKesson	Texas	9
Tesla	Texas	65
Oracle	Texas	91
Hewlett Packard Enterprise	Texas	123
CBRE Group	Texas	126
Charles Schwab	Texas	188
KLA Corporatio	Michigan	474
Parsons	Virginia	733
Kaiser Aluminum	Tennessee	906
Norton Life Synanted	Arizona	917
Woodward Inc.	Colorado	972

Capital Projects

One of the negatives of the state is that it hasn't been investing in capital projects like roads, dams, and bridges. As a result, California now ranks 46th in the nation in terms of per capita spending on capital projects:

7.33 Capital Projects, Selected States Per Capita Spending

State	Rank	Per Million Population
Georgia	2	34.2
Texas	6	27.2
South Carolina	27	21.6
North Carolina	28	18.7
Florida	31	5.9
California	46	2.6

Source: Site Selection Magazine

Best and Worst States for Business

At one time, every business wanted to be in California because it welcomed all businesses and had an enormous growth in population. Now, unfortunately, California is ranked No. 50 as the worst state in the nation to do business, and its nemeses, Texas and Florida, are in the No. 1 and 2 positions.

7.34 Best and Worst States for Business

State	Rank
Texas	1
Florida	2
North Carolina	4
South Carolina	6
Georgia	9
California	50

Source: Chief Executive Magazine

California's Taxes

California's obnoxious tax rates do not sit well with business (along with its labor union friendships and very liberal governments).

7.35 Business Tax Climate Index for Business

State	Rank
Florida	4
North Carolina	11
Texas	14
South Carolina	31
Georgia	32
California	**48**
New York	49
New Jersey	50

Source: Tax Foundation

Public School Ranking

New York and New Jersey may rank near the bottom on business environment, but they shine in "public school ranking." Unfortunately, California is 35th in quality and **50th in Safety.**

7.36 Public School Ranking

State	Score	Quality Rank	Safety Rank
New Jersey	64	3	19
New York	56	11	16
Florida	55	14	20
Texas	49	31	13
California	**42**	**35**	**50**
Georgia	46	36	27
North Carolina	46	37	29
South Carolina	39	42	48

Source: Tax Foundation

There appears to be a correlation between inclement winter temperatures and the quality of public schools:

7.37 Top Ten Quality Ranking
Public School Ranking

State	Rank	Mean Temperature in Winter
Massachusetts	1	27.4
Connecticut	2	28.5
New Jersey	3	33.0
New Hampshire	4	21.1
Virginia	5	36.8
Wisconsin	6	17.2
Minnesota	7	12.4
Maryland	8	34.7
Illinois	9	28.3
North Dakota	10	19.4

Source: NOAA Nat'l Climatic Data Center

Economic Outlook Rankings

Finally, with all the factors accounted for, the overall outlook for California places it in 48th position, lagging only by New York and New Jersey:

7.38 Outlook: Economic Rankings, 2022

State	Rank
North Carolina	2
Florida	8
Texas	11
Georgia	15
South Carolina	26
California	48
New Jersey	49
New York	50

Source: Rich States, Poor States

In the words of Al Jolson in 1921:

> California, here I come
> Right back where I started from
> Where bowers of flowers
> Bloom in the spring
> Each morning at dawning
> Birdies sing at everything
> A sunkissed miss said, "Don't be late!"
> That's why I can hardly wait
> Open up that golden gate
> California, here I come

California's Golden Gates remain open for business.

CHAPTER 8

Texas: A State Worth Bragging About

"Texas is a state of mind. Texas is an obsession. Above all, Texas is a nation in every sense of the word."

—John Steinbeck

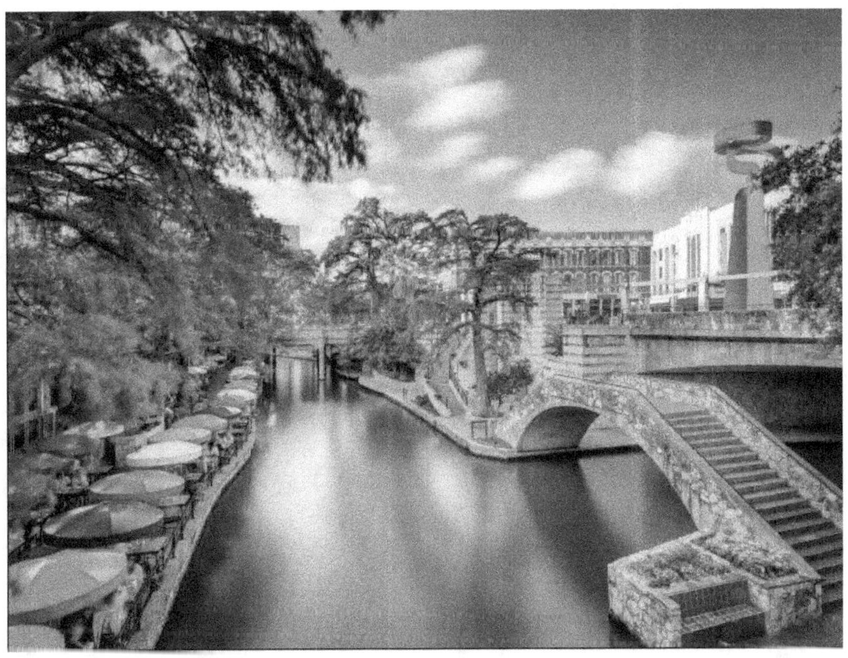

This is a wonderful pictorial of the San Antonio River Walk. Unfortunately, it is a short walk and looks absolutely nothing like the rest of Texas.

What Texas is is jobs. Lots of them and more coming every day. It's a state that may not suit everyone's politics but it certainly is an economic machine that does please a lot of folks, whether you lean right or left.

When the **big recession of 2008-2011** virtually crippled California and Florida, Texas just kept rolling along and then, when the nation recovered, Texas set the pace for new jobs.

8.2 Population Gain and Employment Texas, California, Florida, 2000–2020

Year	Population change Percentage	Employment Change Percentage
Texas		
2000–2010	**20.5%**	**9.5%**
2010–2020	**15.8%**	**17.9%**
California		
2000–2010	9.8%	-3.0%
2010–2020	5.1%	12.1%
Florida		
2000–2010	17.4%	0.8%
2010–2020	13.9%	19.6%
United States		
2000–2010	9.7%	7.4%
2010-2020	7.4%	8.9%

Source: Bureau of Labor Statisticis

Looking at three traditional drivers of the economy—manufacturing, leisure and hospitality, and professional and business services—Texas led the way.

8.3 Economic Drivers
Texas, California, Florida, 2000–2020

						Percent Change	
Year	2000	2010	2020	2000–2010	2010–2020	2000–2010	2010–2020
Manufacturing							
Texas	1,070,200	823,900	861,300	(246,300)	37,400	–23%	5%
California	1,876,200	1,248,400	1,259,500	(627,800)	11,100	–33%	1%
Florida	474,300	309,800	379,400	(164,500)	69,600	–35%	22%
Professional and Business Services							
Texas	1,135,300	1,321,000	1,808,400	185,700	487,400	16%	37%
California	2,278,700	2,112,900	2,622,300	(165,800)	509,400	–7%	24%
Florida	945,000	1,048,200	1,392,300	103,200	344,100	11%	33%
Leisure and Hospitality							
Texas	827,800	1,027,100	1,216,400	199,300	189,300	24%	18%
California	1,355,000	1,526,200	1,358,300	171,200	(167,900)	13%	–11%
Florida	873,900	944,700	1,037,600	70,800	92,900	8%	10%
Total							
Texas	9,566,000	10,476,400	12,352,400	910,400	1,876,000	**10%**	**18%**
California	14,796,500	14,351,000	16,090,700	(445,500)	1,739,700	–3%	12%
Florida	7,145,800	7,200,900	8,615,200	55,100	1,414,300	1%	20%

Source: Bureau of Labor Statistics

The unemployment rate in Texas was continuously below that of the nation throughout the recession and bounced back rapidly and almost ignored COVID. Its unemployment rate now is 3.9%.

8.4 Unemployment Rate
State of Texas, 2010–2022

Year	Unemployment Rate
2010	8.1%
2011	8.1%
2012	7.0%
2013	6.4%
2014	5.1%
2015	4.5%
2016	4.8%
2017	4.1%
2018	3.8%
2019	3.5%
2020	6.9%
2021	4.8%
2022	3.9%

Source: Bureau of Labor Statistics

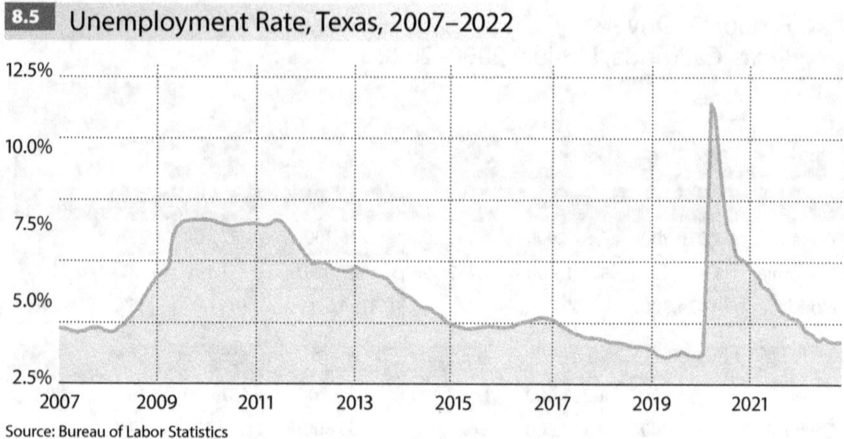

8.5 Unemployment Rate, Texas, 2007–2022

Source: Bureau of Labor Statistics

In terms of labor productivity, Texas just barely comes in positive. "Labor productivity," or output per hour, is calculated by dividing an index of real output by an index of hours worked by all persons.

8.6 Productivity
Selected Major States, 2022

State	Productivity
Washington	6.4%
California	4.2%
Texas	0.7%
Florida	−0.5%
New York	1.8%

Source: BLS

An In-Depth Look at the Population

Population change is a combination of births, deaths, and domestic and international migration. Texas has a fairly stable record of the percentages of those four items. On the following exhibit, we show the four items in the 1990-2020 timeframe.

Typically, 50% of the Texas population is the result of births minus deaths. In the past decade, there were twice as many births as deaths. That's a function of a young population. The other half of the population gain was the result of a combination of domestic and international migration.

8.7 Population – Components of Change State of Texas, 1990–2010

Source of Change	1990-1999	2000-2010	2010-2020
Natural Increase			
Births	3,025,567	3,568,617	3,962,570
Deaths	1,254,005	1,444,493	1,935,156
Net Natural Increase	1,771,562	2,124,124	1,935,156
Migration			
Domestic	569,957	848,702	1,303,879
International	715,420	957,656	869,640
Total Migration	1,285,377	1,806,358	2,173,519
Total Population Change	**3,056,939**	**3,930,482**	**4,108,675**
Percent of Total			
Net Natural Increase	58%	54%	48%
Domestic Migration	19%	22%	31%
International Migration	23%	24%	21%
Total	100%	100%	100%

Source: State of Texas

The key demographic item that has allowed Texas to grow its population much faster than California is **domestic migration**. In the past decade, Texas had a net domestic in-migration of 1.3 million people. Conversely, California had a net outflow of 1.4 million people. They didn't all move to Texas but a big chunk of them did.

Fortunately for California, it continued to be popular to the international market and added more than 1.3 million international migrants, substantially more than Texas.

8.8 Components of Change California, 2010–2020

Category	Population	Percent
Births	4,950,604	
Deaths	2,623,457	
Births–Deaths	2,327,147	101.7%
Migration		
Domestic	**(1,384,171)**	
International	1,344,854	
Total	(39,317)	–1.7%
Total	2,287,830	
Annual	228,783	

Source: California Dept. of Finance

Ethnicity in Texas

In terms of ethnicity, and looking into the future, the Hispanic population is projected to add 14.0 million persons, the Asian (and other) almost six million, and the black population a mere 1.7 million. The non-Hispanic white population will barely add 7.0% to its base, less than one million persons.

These projections, through 2040, are based on the assumption that net migration will be equal to that of the 2000 to 2010 period.

Thus, in the 2010 to 2040 period, 62% of the total population change will be Hispanic, 26% Asian (and other), 8% black, and a very meager 4% non-Hispanic white. Slowly, but surely, the Hispanics are reclaiming Texas for themselves. Thus, the Treaty of Hildago, signed in 1846, may be moot.

8.9 Ethnicity Projections State of Texas, 2020–2040

Ethnicity	2000	2020	2040
Non-Hispanic White	52.4%	40.3%	32.5%
Hispanic	32.0%	40.2%	42.4%
Asian	2.7%	5.4%	9.3%
Black	11.5%	12.2%	13%
Other	1.4%	1.9%	3.2%
Total	100.0%	100.0%	100.0%

Source: State of Texas

Texas Education

Texas has made major strides in education in the past 30 years. Historically, it has been a laggard in K-12 education, particularly for minorities. Since 1990, there has been a major improvement in both high school and college attendance with particular advances in the Hispanic and black population.

The black population has seen high school achievement advance from 66% to 91% and college advancement from 12% to 29%.

The Hispanic population, similarly, has seen its high school advancement rise from 45% to 70% and college from 7% to 18%.

Obviously, there is a long way to go for blacks and Hispanics to achieve parity with non-Hispanic whites and the Asian population, but they are making progress. Asians, as usual, lead the pack.

8.10 Education Levels, State of Texas, 1990–2010

	High School or Higher			College or Higher		
	1990	2010	2020	1990	2010	2020
Non-Hispanic White	82%	92%	95%	25%	34%	42%
Black	66%	86%	91%	12%	20%	29%
Hispanic	45%	60%	70%	7%	12%	18%
Asian and Other	79%	87%	89%	41%	46%	62%

Source: American Community Survey

The three states that we have focused on are California, Texas, and Florida. Looking at those three leads to the conclusion that Texas is a youthful state, with a median age signicantly lower than the other two and with a considerably lower percentage of its population over age 65.

That leads to a conclusion that their costs associated with healthcare for older folks are substantially lower than in the other two states, and, from experience, we know that California's healthcare costs are significanlty higher than in Florida or Texas.

8.11 Median Age and Percent over Age 65
Selected States, 2020

State	Median Age	Percent Over Age 65
Texas	34.8	13.2%
California	36.7	15.2%
Florida	42.2	21.3%
United States	38.1	16.9%

Source: Census Bureau

The Five Major Metropolitan Areas

Five metropolitan areas comprise two-thirds of the population of Texas: Houston, Dallas/Ft. Worth, Austin, San Antonio, and El Paso.

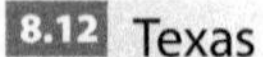

8.12 Texas

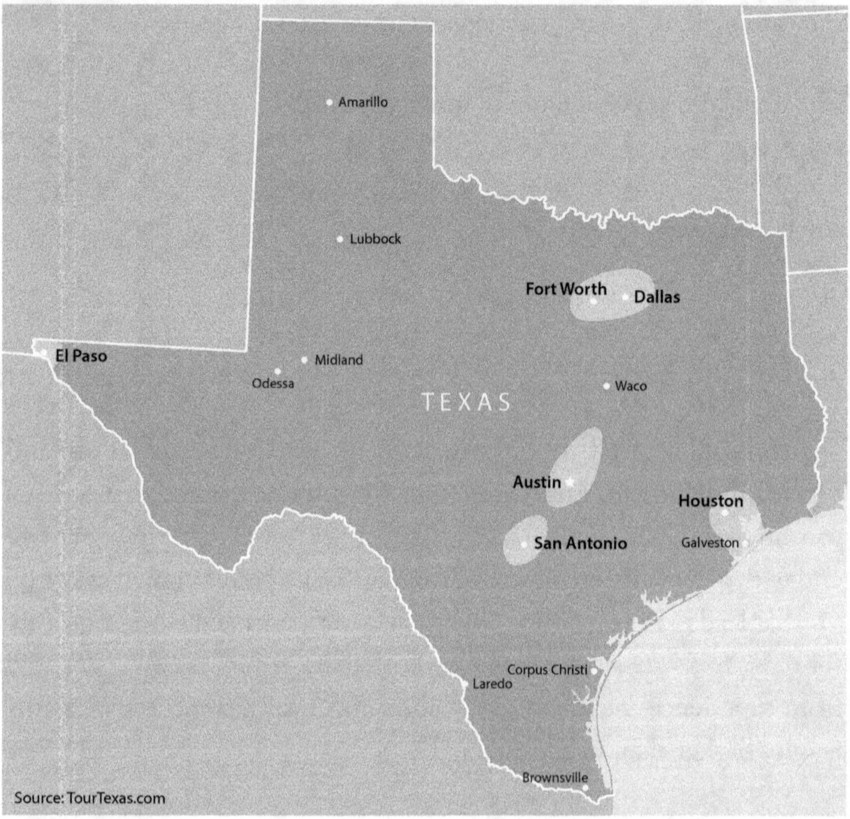

Source: TourTexas.com

Dallas/Ft. Worth and Houston are battling it out for first place in the population competition, both in the range of six million population. Well behind them are San Antonio, Austin, and El Paso in that order. Most have doubled or nearly doubled their population in the past 30 years, except El Paso, which just seems to mosey along.

In total, Texas has added 77% to its population base in the 1800 to 2010 timeframe. Big numbers, but the increase has slowed down and the state has added only 4.0 million population in the past two decades.

8.13 Population Change
Major Metropolitan Areas, Texas, 1980–2020

Metropolitan Area	1980	2000	2020	Change 1980–2000	Change 2000–2020	Percent Change 1980–2000	Percent Change 2000–2020
Big Five							
Dallas/Ft. Worth	3,017,230	6,426,214	7,573,136	3,408,984	1,146,922	113%	18%
Houston	2,424,000	5,920,416	7,066,131	3,496,416	1,145,715	144%	19%
San Antonio	1,124,819	2,142,508	2,509,660	1,017,689	367,152	90%	17%
Austin	585,051	1,716,289	2,227,083	1,131,238	510,794	193%	30%
El Paso	480,000	800,647	844,124	320,647	43,477	67%	5%
Total	**7,631,100**	**17,006,074**	**20,220,134**	**9,374,974**	**3,214,060**	**123%**	**19%**
Other Counties	6,598,091	8,139,487	8,925,371	1,541,396	785,884	110%	23%
Texas	14,229,191	25,145,561	29,145,505	10,916,370	3,999,944	77%	14%

Source: U.S. Census

As you look at the proportional share of the population gains from 1980 to 2020, 84% was in those five major metropolitan areas. It is part of the urbanization of Texas. In 2010, Dallas and Houston accounted for 50% of the population, but 58% of the change in that 30-year period.

Dallas/Ft. Worth

With a population bulging over seven million, Dallas/Ft. Worth would be the 13th largest state in the nation, about the same size as the state of Washington. The major difference there is that Dallas/Ft. Worth will keep on a strong, growing path while Washington will just keep moving along.

In this nation, there are five major distribution points, all anchored by enormous airports: Atlanta, Chicago, Denver, Los Angeles, and Dallas/Ft. Worth. All six have post-COVID enplanements of more than 25 million annually (i.e., number of people boarding). Dallas/Ft. Worth is solidly in second place with 30 million enplanements annually in 2021. Just for the record, that's 75,000 people per day.

Those are post-COVID enplanements. Pre-COVID are much higher:

8.14 Busiest Airports, United States, 2021

No.	Airport	Metro	Enplanements	Pre-COVID 2019
1	Hartsfield	Atlanta	36,676,010	53,505,795
2	Dallas/Ft. Worth	Dallas/Ft. Worth	30,005,266	35,778,573
3	Denver	Denver	28,645,527	33,592,945
4	O'Hare	Chicago	26,350,976	40,871,223
5	LAX	Los Angeles	23,663,410	42,624,050

Source: U.S. Dept. of Transportation

Dallas/Ft. Worth is a business mega-metro. It is home to more than 100,000 businesses and has 1,500 corporate headquarters. It ranks fourth in the nation in *Fortune* magazine's list of corporate headquarters. Dallas is inevitably rated among the very best places in the nation to do business and start a business.

It has a remarkable number of world-class cultural and recreational structures including the Cowboys' stadium, American Airlines Arena, the Meyerson Symphony Center, the Nasher Sculpture Center, and the Perot Museum of Nature and Science. There appears to be an endless number of billionaires in Dallas who just love to have their names on buildings.

Houston

Make no mistake. There is only one Houston in the world. That may be a good thing. It is the city with no zoning and, as far as I can tell, no rules about anything. It is solidly the oil and gas capital of the nation and may be near the top in healthcare services.

It is hot, humid, often smelly, and downright inhospitable. And it is all-business.

It is No. 4 in the nation in terms of gross domestic product (only New York, Los Angeles, and Chicago are ahead of it).

It is the energy capital of the world. Half of the economic activity in the metropolitan area is linked to oil and gas production and exploration. Six of the top 20 employers are energy related, including Exxon, Shell, and Chevron. It has the second highest concentration of engineers in the nation, second only to Silicon Valley. There are 3,700 energy-related firms in the metropolitan area.

Health services also abound in Houston. There are six major hospitals in Houston and a healthcare system that employs almost 300,000 persons.

It also has an amazing selection of cheap housing. They produce new homes for prices that make you wonder how they do it. Maybe 3D printers.

8.15 Median Sale Price – Existing Single-Family Homes
Major Metropolitan Areas
United States, 4th Quarter 2022

Metropolitan Area	Median Price
Houston	$349,500
Atlanta	$371,200
Austin	$541,600
Dallas/Ft. Worth	$390,100
Denver	$660,000
Las Vegas	$463,500
Phoenix	$474,400
San Diego	$900,000

Source: NAR

It is the third most humid city in the nation, upstaged by only New Orleans and Jacksonville. But all seven million folks who live there suffer through it because it is **employment central**.

Its downfall: flooding. The city is like New Orleans—too easy to be inundated by massive water intrusion. This picture is from Houston's 2017 flood.

Austin

Austin is a delightful blend of academics and government. Both are remarkably resilient to downturns in the economy.

Anchoring the community is the **University of Texas at Austin** with 50,000 students and a faculty and staff of 24,000. It is ranked 12th in the nation of all the large schools in a recent Kiplinger Report. And it is right downtown.

State government is the other mega-player with 70,000 employees (mostly downtown), and that does not include lobbyists or other hangers-on. Austin is the state capital, after all.

UT Austin has become a focal point for a wide range of scientific and professional business services that rely on the brainpower at the university. There are some 80,000+ persons engaged in information, scientific, and technical services.

It is probably the most attractive of all the big metros in Texas.

Like most of Texas it is gradually becoming a Hispanic enclave. Its white and black population are quickly being supplanted by an Hispanic and Asian population.

8.17 Change in Ethnicity
Austin Metropolitan Area, 1970–2020

Year	White	Hispanic	Asian	Black
1970	73.4%	14.5%	2.0%	11.1%
1990	61.7%	23.0%	3.0%	12.4%
2000	56.4%	28.2%	4.5%	9.3%
2020	47.1%	32.5%	8.9%	6.9%

Souce: Census Bureau

And there appears to be little homelessness there. I have walked their entire downtown and have failed to see any. They must be doing something right.

The climate is quite reasonable—not quite San Diego, but still very acceptable:

8.18 Climate, Selected Metropolitan Areas, 2021

| State | Summer High | Winter Low | Inches of Rain | |
			Summer	Winter
Austin	**97**	**62**	**4.00**	**2.20**
Orlando	97	50	8.05	2.50
Phoenix	107	66	0.06	0.09
San Diego	77	66	0.01	0.022

Source: Wikipedia

San Antonio

San Antonio matches Austin in terms of employment. Both have 900,000 payroll jobs. Those payroll jobs do not include the military, and the military plays a major role in the San Antonio economy.

Uniformed personnel total more than 35,000 and 27,760 full-time civilian personnel. And there are 55,000 retired military living there. Medical services play a large role in the military in San Antonio, and the metro is home to the USAF School of Aerospace Medicine.

There are more than 200,000 veterans living in San Antonio.

8.19 Military Operations, Ft. San Houston, Lackland AFB, Randolph AFB and Camp Bullis Joint Base, San Antonio, 2021

Base	Full-Time DOD	Full-Time Civilian	Part-Time	Total
Army	8,332			8,332
Navy	3,732			3,732
Air Force	21,508			21,508
Coast Guard	122			122
Army Reserve	51			51
Appropriated and Non-Appropriated		27,760	1,624	29,384
Total	**33,745**	**27,760**	**1,624**	**63,129**

Souce: From DOD base structure report 2021

8.20 Best Places for Veterans to Live
WalletHub Survey 100 Metropolitan Area

Factor	San Antonio Score	No. 1	No. 2	No. 3
Employment	62	Durham, NC	Lincoln, NE	Boise
Economy	11	Laredo, TX	Va. Beach, VA	Ft. Worth
Quality of Life	37	San Diego	Orlando	Boise
Health	43	San Jose	Laredo, TX	Fremont, CA

Source: Wallet Hub Survey

Each year, WalletHub conducts an extensive survey of "Best Places for Veterans to Live." San Antonio does well on being economical, but not particularly well on the other factors.

Professional, Science, and Technical Services and information systems along with healthcare employ yet another 250,000 persons.

Another 100,000+ are employed in the tourism sector. San Antonio has a strong draw as a vacation destination because of its River Walk and history.

El Paso

Located at the far west end of Texas, looking at Ciudad Juarez across the border, the sleepy town of El Paso continues to grow by about 10,000 per year.

Like San Antonio, it has a military presence. Ft. Bliss has 33,000 personnel on its 122,000 acres.

El Paso serves as Ciudad Juarez's "shopping center" and, for many, its healthcare. At one time, El Paso was a large apparel manufacturing center, particularly jeans manufacturing, but that went off-shore some time ago. Of the 300,000 jobs in El Paso, only 18,000 are in manufacturing.

Ciudad Juarez, with its crime infestation, has cast a pall over El Paso.

The Department of State assesses crime as "critical" in Ciudad Juarez, with **1,400 persons killed in 2021**. It's still a distant second to Tijuana's 2,000 average. A significant majority of homicides in Juarez are drug cartel related; however, there have been cases in which innocent people are caught in the line of fire, or mistakenly targeted.

As a major drug trafficking corridor, the state of Chihuahua has been contested by two major Transnational Criminal Organizations (TCOs) for years. With more availability of drugs in Juarez, drug use has also increased locally. Carjackings are also a cottage industry.

Having said that, El Paso is ranked as the third safest city in America, just ahead of another border city: San Diego.

8.21 The Safest Cities in America (2021)

Small — Less than 100K			Midsize — 100K–300K			Large — 300K+		
1	Rye	NY	1	Carmel	IN	1	Virginia Beach	VA
2	Broadview Heights	OH	2	Sugar Land	TX	2	Henderson	NV
3	Berkeley Heights	NJ	3	Cary	NC	3	El Paso	TX
4	Norfolk	MA	4	Thousand Oaks	CA	4	San Diego	CA
5	Sparta	NJ	5	Murrieta	CA	5	Honolulu	HI
6	River Vale	NJ	6	Lakewood	NJ	6	Mesa	AZ
7	Sagamore Hills	OH	7	Allen	TX	7	New York	NY
8	Bedford	NY	8	Santa Clarita	CA	8	Santa Ana	CA
9	Clearcreek	OH	9	Irvine	CA	9	Anaheim	CA
10	Hasbrouch Heights	NJ	10	Simi Valley	CA	10	Raleigh	NC

Source: Data provided by AdvisorSmith

El Paso continues to grow thanks to its military component, its substantial retiree base, and its cross-border business.

CHAPTER 9

South Atlantic States: The South Is Rising Again

The first time you leave it can be strange, it can be shocking

Not everybody drives a truck, not everybody drinks sweet tea
Not everybody owns a gun, wears a ball cap, boots and jeans
Not everybody goes to church or watches every NASCAR race
Not everybody knows the words to Ring of Fire or Amazing Grace

Oh, Dixie Land
I hope you understand
And I been away, way too long
And I can't see this world unless I go
Outside my Southern Comfort zone

Brad Paisley

I initially was going to call this chapter "The Deep South," but that would mean I would have had to include states like Louisiana, Tennessee, and Alabama. Instead, I just want to focus on the few states that span from North Carolina to Florida, as they are growing at a pace that places them at the forefront of U.S. economic activity.

Those four states are responsible for almost a quarter of all the population gain in the nation in the past 20 years and are anticipated to keep up the pace in the next 20 years as well:

9.1 Population Change
South Atlantic States, 2000–2040

State	2000	2020	2000–2020		2020	2040	2020–2040	
			Total	%			Total	%
North Carolina	8,049,313	10,439,388	2,390,075	30%	10,439,388	12,660,000	2,220,612	21%
South Carolina	4,012,012	5,118,425	1,106,413	28%	5,118,425	6,350,000	1,231,575	24%
Georgia	8,186,453	10,711,908	2,525,455	31%	10,711,908	12,820,000	2,108,092	20%
Florida	15,982,378	21,538,187	5,555,809	35%	21,538,187	28,890,000	7,351,813	34%
Total	36,230,156	47,807,908	11,577,752	32%	47,807,908	60,720,000	12,912,092	27%
U.S.	281,421,906	331,449,281	50,027,375	18%	331,449,281	331,449,281	50,027,375	15%
Percent of U.S.	13%	14%	23%		14%	18%	26%	

Source: Census Bureau

Exhibit 9.2 clearly shows the population changes from 2000-2020 and projected for 2020-2040 for the four states compared to the nation. The rate of change will slow down somewhat but still be impressive.

9.2 Population Change
South Atlantic States, 2000–2040

State	Percent Change	
	2000–2020	2020–2040
North Carolina	30%	21%
South Carolina	28%	24%
Georgia	31%	20%
Florida	35%	34%
Total	32%	27%
U.S.	18%	15%

Source: Census Bureau

Jobs follow population. In the U.S., two-thirds of all spending and, concomitantly two-thirds of all jobs relate to population growth. Thus, in exhibit 9.3 you can see the massive employment growth in the four South Atlantic states. The job growth in those four states is at a rate double that of the United States (16% compared to 7.0%).

9.3 Employment, South Atlantic States, 2000–2020

State	2000	2020	2000–2020	Percent Change 2000–2020
North Carolina	3,912,000	4,492,900	580,900	15%
South Carolina	1,849,900	2,119,700	269,800	15%
Georgia	4,003,500	4,470,300	466,800	12%
Florida	7,145,800	8,615,200	1,469,400	21%
Total	16,911,200	19,698,100	2,786,900	16%
U.S.	132,718,000	142,475,000	9,757,000	7%
Percent of U.S.	13%	14%	29%	

Source: Census Bureau

In days gone by, the four states (and particularly North Carolina) were meccas for manufacturing, mostly textiles.

Textile mills in the South grew from 160 mills in 1880 to 400 in 1900. The textile industry dominated the South but peaked in 1948 with 1.3 million jobs. And then gradually receded. Between 1997 and 2009, 650 textile mills closed.

Starting in the 2010s, China began to outsource textile industry jobs to the U.S. Hard to believe, but true. Today, the American textile industry is the fourth largest exporter of textile products in the world. There are now two dozen Chinese-owned textile plants in the South.

Of course, efficiencies in the textile industries have been great, and without the benefit of human hands, machines can produce a t-shirt in 30 seconds.

Thus, manufacturing of textiles expanded but manufacturing employment sagged, as it has nationwide. And, of course, the decline in manufacturing includes many more industries than textiles.

9.4 Manufacturing Employment, South Atlantic States, 2000–2020

State	2000	2020	2000–2020	Percent Change 2000–2020
North Carolina	747,500	456,800	(290,700)	–39%
South Carolina	333,000	246,900	(86,100)	–26%
Georgia	527,600	386,300	(141,300)	–27%
Florida	474,300	379,400	(94,900)	–20%
Total	2,082,400	1,469,400	(613,000)	–29%
U.S.	17,181,000	12,199,000	(4,982,000)	–29%
Percent of U.S.			**12%**	

Source: Census Bureau

Fortunately, Professional and Business Services employment has been the driving force in the four South Atlantic states, adding almost 1.0 million jobs in the past two decades, thereby indicating a major category shift in employment.

9.5 Professional and Business Employment
South Atlantic States, 2000–2020

State	2000	2020	2000–2020	Percent Change 2000–2020
North Carolina	422,700	652,900	230,200	54%
South Carolina	196,100	289,200	93,100	47%
Georgia	550,900	716,200	165,300	30%
Florida	945,000	1,392,300	447,300	47%
Total	2,114,700	3,050,600	935,900	**44%**
U.S.	16,893,000	20,710,000	3,817,000	23%
Percent of U.S.	13%	15%	**25%**	

Source: Census Bureau

In addition to the Professional and Business Services, the South Atlantic states have become meccas of vehicle and vehicle parts manufacturing:

9.6 Vehicle and Vehicle Parts Manufacturing, Georgia, 2022

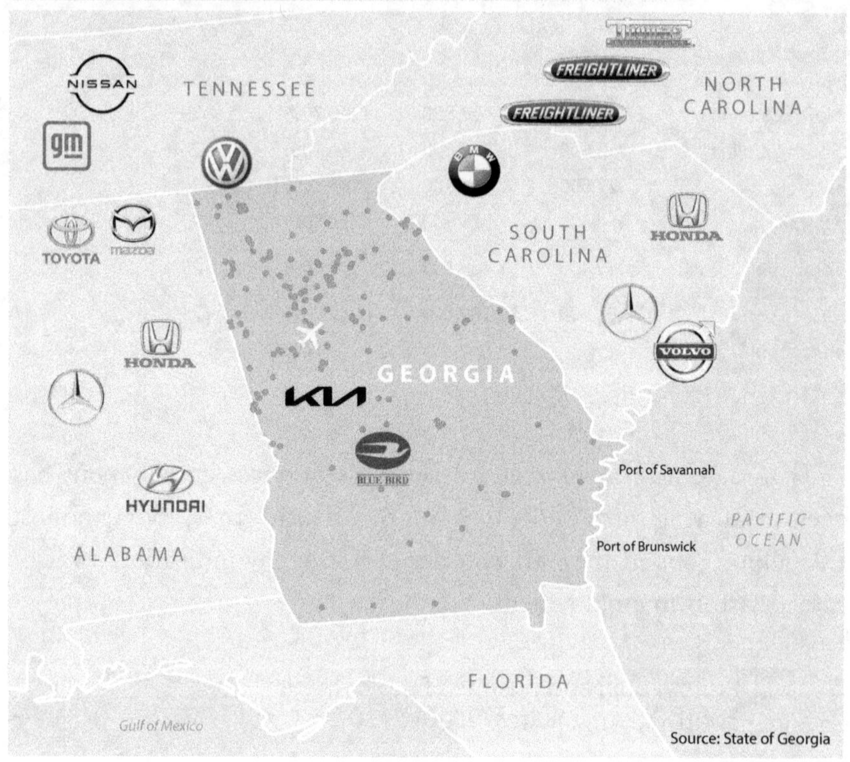

A partial listing of vehicle manufacturing plants is shown in Exhibit 9.7:

9.7 Vehicle Manufacturing (Major Employers), South Atlantic States

Georgia	South Carolina	North Carolina
Rivian	Volvo	Freighliner
Kia	Mercedes	VinFast
	BMW	Thomas School Buses
	Honda	
	ZF Transmissions	
	Michelin Tires	

Ethnicity in the South Atlantic States

The predominant minorities in the South Atlantic states are black and Hispanic. Typically the black population has comprised 20-30% of the population in North and South Carolina and Georgia and lesser so in Florida. That ratio has been stable in the past 20 years.

9.8 Black Ethnicity by State
South Atlantic States, 2000–2020

Year	North Carolina	South Carolina	Georgia	Florida	Total
Black Population					
2000	1,737,546	1,185,216	2,393,425	2,335,505	7,651,692
2020	2,140,217	1,280,531	3,320,513	3,246,381	9,987,642
Change	402,671	95,315	927,088	910,876	2,335,950
Percent Change	**23%**	**8%**	**39%**	**39%**	**31%**
Total State Population					
2000	8,049,313	4,012,012	8,186,453	15,982,379	36,230,157
2020	10,439,388	5,118,425	10,711,908	21,538,187	47,807,908
Change	2,390,075	1,106,413	2,525,455	5,555,808	11,577,751
Percent Change	**30%**	**28%**	**31%**	**35%**	**32%**
Black as Percent of State					
2000	22%	30%	29%	15%	**21%**
2020	21%	25%	31%	15%	**21%**

Source: Census Bureau

The major change in ethnicity has been the relative explosion of the **Hispanic population** in all four South Atlantic States. The percentage has almost doubled in the past 20 years and in the next 20 years will approach more than ¼ of the total population in the South Atlantic states.

9.9 Hispanic Ethnicity by State
South Atlantic States, 2000–2020

Year	North Carolina	South Carolina	Georgia	Florida	Total
Hispanic Population					
2000	378,963	95,076	435,227	2,682,715	3,591,981
2020	1,070,000	329,420	1,083,520	5,830,920	8,313,860
Change	691,037	234,344	648,293	3,148,205	4,721,879
Percent Change	**182%**	**246%**	**149%**	**117%**	**131%**
Total State Population					
2000	8,049,313	4,012,012	8,186,453	15,982,379	36,230,157
2020	10,439,388	5,118,425	10,711,908	21,538,187	47,807,908
Change	2,390,075	1,106,413	2,525,455	5,555,808	11,577,751
Percent Change	**30%**	**28%**	**31%**	**35%**	**32%**
Hispanic as Percent of State					
2000	5%	2%	5%	17%	**10%**
2020	10%	6%	10%	27%	**17%**

Source: Census Bureau

The predominant reasons for the expansion of the Hispanic market are mass in-migration from Puerto Rico, Cuba, and South and Central America. And a higher fertility rate in the Hispanic population.

THE FOUR SOUTH ATLANTIC STATES

Let's take a look at the four states:

Florida, the Swamp State

I have been consulting in Florida since the early 1970s and could never figure out how the state exists, economically speaking. The state has 21 million inhabitants and I have no idea what they do for a living. They manufacture nothing; they process nothing; they have no world-class universities; and their weather is abominable (and getting worse). It is hot and humid most of the year. All they have is Disney World, but even that gargantuan effort can't support 21 million people.

Florida's really big selling point is that you can get from New York to Miami in three hours (assuming that the plane doesn't have snow delays in New York).

And they do have a remarkable selection of cruises. Three million passengers a year.

(The best year San Diego ever had was 300,000.)

9.10 What's Good and Bad About Florida

Good	Bad
Atlantic Ocean beaches	Alligators
Cheap everything	Elderly drivers
Great weather, Oct-May	Hurricanes
Cheap housing	Impossible Summers
Disney World, summers	Mosquitoes
Easy to to get to and from New York	Suffocating humidity
Great cruise selection	Swamps

Cost of Living

The cost of living is modest and substantially less than a metropolitan area like San Diego.

9.11 Cost of Living Comparison, Miami and San Diego

Index	Miami	San Diego	Percent Difference	Percent Difference
Overall index	120.6	143.8	23.2	19.2%
Groceries	120	111.9	−8.1	−6.7%
Housing	147.3	222.8	75.5	51.3%
Utilities	106.4	113.0	6.6	6.2%
Transportation	107.8	131.5	23.7	22.0%
Health Care	94.5	104.4	9.9	10.5%
Goods and Services	109.4	109.5	0.1	0.1%

Source: Council for Community and Economic Research

Whereas ConEd's motto was "Dig We Must," Florida's is "Grow We Must." I suspect that Florida is a massive Ponzi scheme. If people stop moving there from New York, the entire economy collapses overnight.

A recent AARP study showed that **25% of the seniors in New York State intend to move** to Florida. The IRS taxpayer migration data shows that in the past decade, more than one million taxpayers moved out of New York. One-third of them moved to Florida. Most brought their bank accounts with them, which is why there is a bank and financial planning firm on every corner in Florida.

The big march to Florida started after World War II. Prior to that, the state got an initial boost from the start of interstate train service in the early 1900s when Henry Flagler created a major intrastate line that went all the way down to Key West. Florida actually had intrastate train service before the Civil War, but much of that was destroyed in the war. Mr. Flagler had a buck or two to spend because he was John D. Rockefeller's partner in Standard Oil.

The auto trains that started in the 1950s from Virginia to Florida actually had an earlier start with trains running from Florida to New York as early as 1910.

Not to belabor the rail history, but the Great Depression dramatically slowed down Florida's expansion until the late 1930s and then was interrupted again by World War II.

In 1963, the railway unions went on strike and caused a massive slowdown of rail travel on the Atlantic seaboard through 1975.

Of course, by that time, jet air travel was available to Florida for rather low prices, making passenger train service somewhat irrelevant. The jet age was a major factor in creating the Gold Coast of Florida with its myriad of hotels and condominiums.

From 1950 to 2021, Florida grew from fewer than 3.0 million to 21.0 million persons today. Since 1980, the state has grown by more than 300,000 persons annually.

Folks over 65 now comprise almost a quarter of the population of Florida, continually edging up with each census. In the past 60 years, the number of seniors has increased 700%.

I should note that the Gold Coast (Dade, Broward, and Palm Beach Counties) are far and away the most expensive areas of Florida.

9.12 Population by Age Group State of Florida, 1960–2020

Year	Under age 18	18–64	65+	Total	Percent over 65
1960	1,681,494	2,714,948	555,118	4,951,560	11%
1980	1,789,875	5,699,487	1,687,961	9,746,961	17%
2000	3,646,450	9,528,724	2,807,650	15,982,824	18%
2020	4,048,632	12,801,379	4,422,335	21,538,187	21%
Change 1960–2020	2,367,138	10,086,431	3,867,217	16,586,627	
Percent Change	141%	372%	697%	335%	

Source: Census Bureau

A major part of Florida's growth is migration—both domestic and international. In the 2010-2020 timeframe, almost 90% of the state's growth was the result of folks moving in.

The Florida population gains can be segmented into **natural increase** (births over deaths) and **domestic migration** and **international migration**. The natural increase is fairly steady. The big change is the proportion of the population gain that is international.

And remember, this is long after the Cuban in-migration. The new international in-migration tends to be both European and Brazilian. Sao Paolo is an eight-hour flight directly north to Miami. And Europe is just a five-hour hop.

When the boom was burgeoning in the early 2000s, there were plane-loads of Europeans being brought to Florida by entities that would sell them new sub-division homes. There were dozens of European magazines published that hyped the Florida experience.

9.13 Components of Population Change (in Percent) State of Florida, 1980–2020

Category	1980–1990	1990–2000	2010–2020
Births	1,614,057	1,931,148	2,190,579
Deaths	1,193,190	1,482,932	1,902,108
Natural Increase	420,867	448,216	288,471
Domestic	2,049,873	1,947,068	1,289,614
International	664,824	649,023	1,107,039
Net Migration	2,770,098	2,596,091	2,396,653
Percent International	24%	25%	46%
Total	3,190,729	3,044,753	2,685,124

Source: Census, Population Division, Estimates of the Components of Resident Change for Counties in Florida (CO-EST2019-COMP-12)

Two-thirds of all of Florida's population gains are in four metropolitan areas: the Gold Coast, Orlando, Tampa/St. Petersburg, and Jacksonville. The other 34 counties share one-third of the population gains.

9.14 Population Change
Major Metros, State of Florida, 2000–2020

State	2000	2020	Change Number	Change Percent
Miami-Ft. Lauderdale	5,007,988	6,138,333	1,130,345	23%
Orlando	1,644,563	2,673,376	1,028,813	63%
Tampa/St. Pete	2,396,013	3,175,276	779,263	33%
Jacksonville	1,122,750	1,605,848	483,098	43%
Total	10,171,314	13,592,833	3,421,519	34%
Balance	5,808,686	7,997,167	2,188,481	38%
Total	15,980,000	21,590,000	5,610,000	35%
Big 4 as Percent of Total	36%	63%	61%	

Source: Census Bureau

The Fraser Institute routinely rates the states on Economic Freedom, a rating that includes property rights, taxes, government spending, labor market freedom, and legal systems. **Florida ranks No. 2 in the nation**. Basically, a good place to do business.

9.15 Economic Freedom
The South Atlantic States
United States, 2018

State	Score	Rank
Florida	7.73	2
Georgia	7.27	7
North Carolina	6.95	11
South Carolina	6.11	30

Source: Fraser Institute

A substantial part of Florida's wealth relates to transfer payments generated from industrial centers in the North.

Each winter, almost 1.0 million snowbirds congregate in Florida.

As a final note, Florida has some of the largest universities in the nation, headed up by the University of Central Florida with 70,000 students, Florida International University with 56,000 students, and the University of Florida with 55,000 students.

THE FOUR BIG METROS

The Gold Coast (Miami, Ft. Lauderdale, Palm Beach)

I am tempted to say that the Gold Coast is tarnished, but that just isn't true. It continues to be an enormous draw to foreign civilians like Brazilians, Europeans, Central and South Americans, and New Yorkers. And they have created a broad range of retail and culinary establishments.

Within the Gold Coast, there are some differences in demographics. For instance, 69% of the population in Dade County is Hispanic compared to only 32% in Broward and 23% in Palm Beach County.

The **median age** is the highest of the three in Palm Beach County at 45.

In terms of household size, the average is highest in Dade County, followed by Broward and Palm Beach County.

Statistically speaking, the Gold Coast counties get richer and more educated as you go north. Thus, in Palm Beach County 33% of the population has a bachelor's degree or higher compared to Dade County's 26%.

9.16 Evidence of Affluence, Gold Coast Counties, 2020

County	Dade	Broward	Palm Beach
Major City	Miami	Ft. Lauderdale	Palm Beach
Percent over 65	16.9%	17.5%	24.5%
Percent Hispanic	69.1%	32.0%	23.0%
Average Household Size	2.83	2.62	2.51

Source: 2020 Census

Also, home ownership increases substantially as you go northward. In Dade County, 52% own a home compared to 69% in Palm Beach County, and in Palm Beach County 61% of owned homes have no mortgage compared to 52% in Dade County.

I also looked at the great state of California and the nation to see how Florida compares. The most poignant differential is that in California only 21% of homeowners have no mortgage compared to 35% in Florida, but you could have guessed that anyhow. Also, in California 27% of the households have an income over $100,000 compared to 18% in Florida. The costs of living in California compared to Florida mandate higher incomes. It all evens out in the end.

9.17 Evidence of Affluence, Gold Coast Counties, 2020

Category	Dade	Broward	Palm Beach
Bachelors Degree or Higher	31.7%	34.3%	38.0%
Median Household Income	$68,874	$64,522	$57,815
Percent of households with more than $100,000 income	29.0%	28.3%	28.3%
Percent of homeowners without a mortgage	54.0%	60.0%	61.0%
Own their home	51.9%	62.7%	69.4%

Source: Census Bureau

Orlando

The world's playground. Orlando gets more tourists than any city in the U.S. (maybe the world). In 2022, Orlando played host to a record 57 million persons. That pales in comparison to the pre-COVID visitations of 75 million in 2019. Also, in 2019 there were 6.5 million international visitors compared to 2.0 million in 2022.

One of every three jobs in Orlando is tourism related. Orlando has 450 hotels/motels and 129,000 rooms (second only to Las Vegas).

9.18 Main Tourist Attractions, Orlando

Big Time	Side Shows (Partial List)
Disney World	Chocolate Kingdom
Magic Kingdom	Screamin' Gator Zip Line
Epcot	Dinosaur World
Animal Kingdom	Gatorland
Hollywood Studio	Discovery Cove
Universal Studios	Madame Tussauds
Legoland	Wet 'n Wild
Seaworld	Ripley's Believe It or Not

Its convention center is one of the largest in the nation with 7.0 million square feet. The center averages 115 conventions and tradeshows and more than 1.5 million attendees each year.

TAMPA/ST. PETERSBURG

I have visited the Tampa/St. Petersburg area numerous times over the years and cannot figure out what drives the economy there. It is highly possible that assisted living, memory care, and other health services are the base of the local economy. The statistics show that one out of every four jobs is in health services, but I think it is higher than that.

The bright spot, of late, is the resuscitation of downtown Tampa. With several new office buildings and residential towers, five museums, the Florida Aquarium, and a vibrant convention center, it has come to life.

I should mention that the west coast of Florida from Tampa/St. Petersburg south is a collection of very nice resort cities including Sarasota, Fort Myers, Sanibel Island, Captiva Island, and Pensacola Beach.

Jacksonville

Now there's a normal city. It is the gateway to Florida, just across the state line from Georgia. It has a normal complement of population and a normal distribution of jobs.

It is a water-related town with the largest deepwater port in the South and is the largest auto importer on the East Coast. It is the largest transportation and distribution center in the state. It is also a military town with 30,000 uniformed personnel and 20,000 civilians attached to the military.

It is named after General Andrew Jackson who, incidentally, never visited the city.

And its primary claim to fame is that it has the largest urban park system in the United States with 111,000 acres of parks (so sayeth the Chamber of Commerce).

Not your typical Florida tourism town, but a nice place to work and live.

Conclusion: If living in a year-round, screened-in environment is your thing, Florida is definitely the place for you. If you like to live really cheap, Florida is also the place for you. Little by little, Florida is turning into an enclave for Europeans, Brazilians, and New Yawkers, and those three in-migrant groups will keep Florida growing indefinitely.

One last thought: Florida is also a great place to buy used Cadillacs in great condition as the aging population inevitably and reluctantly tosses their car keys to CarMax.

Georgia—The Peach State

Georgia's peaches are somewhat sweeter than the politics in Georgia. Despite that truism, Georgia is a business state. It is the long-term home of Home Depot, UPS, Delta Airlines, Coca-Cola, and numerous other major firms.

It is a job machine. The five basic industries of Georgia are all doing well.

9.20 Employment Highlights, Georgia, 2022

Category	2021	2022	Change	%
Professional and Business Services	749,900	784,500	34,600	4.6%
Leisure and Hospitality	470,900	505,000	34,100	7.2%
Trade, Transportation and Utilities	988,000	1,011,000	23,000	2.3%
Information	130,000	140,500	10,500	8.1%
Manufacturing	405,200	414,200	9,000	2.2%

Source: BLS

And Georgia is a college state. Its largest university in terms of enrollment is Kennesaw State with 36,000+ undergraduate students, followed by the University of Georgia and Georgia State.

9.21 Major Universities, Georgia

University	Locale	Undergraduate Enrollment
University of Georgia	Athens	30,166
Georgia State	Atlanta	28,085
Georgia Institute of Technology	Atlanta	17,447
Emory	Atlanta	6,978
Spelman	Atlanta	2,400
Morehouse	Atlanta	2,550
Kennesaw State Univeresity	Kennesaw	36,284
Clayton State University	Morrow	3,680

Georgia is the home of nine **historically black colleges and universities (HBCU),** including Morehouse College, Morehouse School of Medicine, and Spelman College.

Besides the dominant city of Atlanta, the top five things that Georgia is known for are:

- Savannah, a great historic city
- Great peaches

- Okefenokee Swamp
- Georgia peanuts
- "The World of Coca-Cola"

South Carolina

South Carolina doesn't get much press, but it is known for its **beaches, golf courses, and historic districts.** It ranks 40th in size and 23rd in population. Its most influential cities are Charleston, Myrtle Beach, Columbia, and Greenville.

It is a tourism state anchored by Charleston. I have spent many a day strolling around Charleston's architecturally delightful streets with its Victorian homes and exceptionally good restaurants.

It greets more than 7.0 million visitors every year, which translates into a $10 billion economic impact.

And, in addition, Charleston has 17 golf courses and a climate that allows you to play all-year round.

North Carolina

If I were to focus on what is really good in North Carolina, I'd have to say No. 1: its universities. Clustered around Raleigh-Durham are the University of North Carolina, Wake Forest, and Duke.

9.22 Major Universities, North Carolina

University	Locale	Undergraduate Enrollment
University of North Carolina	Raleigh	36,000
University of North Carolina	Charlotte	30,000
University of North Carolina	Chapel Hill	30,000
Duke	Durham	16,000
Wake Forest	Winston–Salem	18,000

In addition, North Carolina is a major manufacturing state with an amazing number of Fortune 500 firms in a myriad of industries. Among the largest are IBM, Smithfield Foods, Pfizer, R.J. Reynolds, and GE-Hitachi Nuclear Energy America.

9.23 Major Manufacturers, North Carolina

Industry	Manufacturers
Aerospace	Lockheed Martin, GE Aviation, Honda Jet
Automotive trucks	Freightliner, Daimler, Caterpillar
Food Processing	Tyson, Campbell's, Smithfield
Biotechnology	Merck, Novo Nordisk, Fuji

North Carolina also boasts the largest Research and Development park in the nation (the **Research Triangle**). Founded in the 1950s, it now has 7,000+ acres, 375 companies, and more than 60,000 employees.

North Carolina also boasts that it is the **"furniture capital"** of the nation with a 35,000+ workforce in furniture manufacturing—the largest in the U.S.

North Carolina is also a banking state. It is, in fact, the second largest banking state in the U.S., trailing only New York. (California is No. 3.)

North Carolina is a happening place.

The South is rising again.

CHAPTER 10

Moving Up Through Sharing: Prepare for an Amazing Change in World Prosperity

In the mid-1990s, fewer than 1% of the global population was online. Now 66% of the world is connected. In the past three years alone, more than a billion more people have come online.

Since the end of World War II, the number of countries in the world has more than tripled, from 46 to nearly 200. Most of these new countries are weak and lack energy, resources, food, and advanced technology. Political scientist Arjun Chowdhury states "that two thirds of the new countries cannot provide basic services to their people without international help."

The primary theme of this book is the remarkable changes that are going to take place worldwide during next the few decades. Those changes relate primarily to the substantial number of countries that are going to move from developing status to Second World status.

This is going to happen because these countries will turn to manufacturing and learn other viable skills that will allow them to join the middle class, not unlike the U.S. did 100+ years ago.

The great news is that the U.S. had to develop the machinery that allowed the population to get jobs that paid sufficiently for them to buy homes and cars and get educated. Today, the machinery and business practices are in place, so the Third World countries just need the opportunity to use them. And it is happening and will happen with great vigor in the next few decades.

Further, education is increasingly better in these countries and, in most of the countries, females can be educated along with the males.

As households in these countries increase their incomes, they move toward middle-class status and want to have all the capitalistic "goodies" that come with being middle class. To do that, they have to reduce the number of children. In the exhibit below, look at the remarkable **decline in fertility** in these seven societies in a 40-year period. Several are approaching the fertility rates in the First World countries.

10.1 Total Fertility[1]
Major Second and Third World Countries, 1980–2020

Country	Change 1980–2020	1980–1985	2015–2020
Philippines	–118%	5.20	2.50
Mexico	–141%	6.00	2.49
India	–117%	4.85	2.24
Iraq	–100%	7.35	3.68
Pakistan	–81%	6.44	3.55
Egypt	–65%	5.49	3.33
Sub-Sahara Africa	–42%	6.72	4.72

1. Females aged 15–44

Source: United Nations 2017 Population Projections

Concomitantly, the **income per capita** has exploded. In most cases, the income has increased 400-500% or more within a 40-year period.

10.2 Annual Income Per Capita[1]
Major Second and Third World Countries, 1980–2020

Country	Change 1980–2020	1980	2020
Egypt	600%	$500	$3,000
Ghana	582%	$402	$2,340
India	722%	$266	$1,920
Kenya	458%	$402	$1,840
Pakistan	419%	$303	$1,270
Philippines	441%	$778	$3,430
Viet Nam	659%	$402	$2,650

1. U.S. Dollars

Source: World Bank

And finally, the improvements in these developing countries have enabled their citizens to live longer with some remarkable increase in longevity in the past 50 years:

10.3 Life Expectancy, Third World Countries

	In Years	
Country	1970	2020
United States	70	79
Egypt	51	72
Ghana	49	64
India	46	70
Kenya	51	67
Pakistan	51	68
Philippines	60	71
Viet Nam	62	76

Source: United Nations Research

In Jeffrey Sachs's new book, *How Poverty Ends*, he notes that according to World Bank, 36% of the global population was living in extreme poverty in 1990; this proportion declined to 10% in 2015.

And now as we proceed through a new decade, we can once again focus on our great nation's role in the world and its incredible opportunities to move many of the 190 nations in the world closer to First World status and even more from Third World to Second World status.

First, a definition:

A **First World country** is one that is literate and capitalistic (U.S. and the European Union).

A **Second World** country is mostly literate and has many of the elements of capitalism but is usually a blend of capitalism and socialism (i.e., China, India).

A **Third World** country typically has an illiterate population with meager education and is rarely capitalistic and often is governed by dictatorship (most of Africa).

With more than three-quarters of a century to go in the 2000s, we will see some remarkable changes take place, just as we saw in the 19th and 20th century.

Prior to the second half of the 19th century, the world hadn't changed much for thousands of years. Prior to that time period, humanity's total focus was on survival. Virtually the entirety of the economies was focused on producing sufficient food for survival.

Then, in the **first half of the 20th century**, what are now First World countries entered a new era of creativity that produced:

- Railroads
- Telephones
- Electric lighting
- Automobiles
- Typewriters
- Large-scale manufacturing
- Modern educational systems
- Sewer and water systems and flush toilets
- Central heating

Then, in the **second half of the 20th century**, First World countries created

- Mass agriculture
- Air conditioning
- Airplanes
- Cruise ships
- Nuclear fission (and bombs)
- Modern weapons of war
- Radio/television

- Movies with talking
- "Modern medicine" (including penicillin)
- Rudimentary computers
- Social security and life insurance

In the **second half of the 20th century**, First World countries created:

- Major advances in medicine (think Salk, Sabin, et al.)
- Modern computers
- Cell phones
- The Internet and social media
- Highway systems
- Large-scale tourism and hotels and resorts
- Modern housing for the masses
- Drones
- Artificial Intelligence
- Modern banking and lending

Each of these three time periods resulted in major increases in speed.

And now that we are in **Century 21**, we cannot begin to envision what lies ahead in the world of creativity and the betterment of mankind. Just the advent of AI (artificial intelligence) will have a massive impact on education and literacy and productivity.

Unfortunately, relatively few of the 190 countries in the world share in the wonderful things we have created. Not yet, anyhow.

The thesis of this book is that because of the **inventiveness** and **capitalistic nature** of First World countries, most of the Second and Third World countries are now able to look into the lifestyle of those who live in First World countries and will gradually move forward with modernization and, most importantly, capitalism.

In many of these countries, as the populace achieves higher levels of education, most dictatorial leadership will be overthrown. In years to come, it will become **less possible** for dictatorial leaders to block out the Internet and social media and the charitable foundations that are willing to contribute billions of dollars to improve the lifestyles of developing countries.

According to Jon Temin of the U.S. State Department, leadership changes rapidly in developing countries. Of the 49 leaders in power in sub-Saharan Africa at the beginning of 2015, only 22 of them remained in power in 2019.

It will be the job of the governments to create the conditions for success. It is the government's duty to lead the public through a process of diagnosing the problem and identifying a shared plan for solving it. This is fundamentally an act of public education.

There are six critical areas where the First World nations will be able to impart their skills on the "move-up" of Second and Third World countries:

- Education
- Medical care
- Food production
- Capitalism
- Governance
- Financing and money management

The Chinese Example

China provides a classic story of a country that less than half a century ago was a Third World nation and now is clearly a Second World nation, and it is not inconceivable that it can achieve First World status by the end of this century.

In the past quarter century, household incomes in China have increased five times and China's gross national product has similarly increased more than 10 times in that same time frame. Obviously it continues to be socialistic, but it has many of the positive elements of capitalism.

Human Development Index

The basis for determining the ranking of countries into First, Second, and Third World status is a function of the United Nations research division. The ranking determines what they have designated the **Human Development Index**.

In this evaluative process, the United Nations segments 188 counties of the world into First, Second, and Third World countries. According to their index, half of the countries in the world are Third World countries with a current population of almost 4.0 billion people.

10.4 Population and Status
First, Second, Third World Countries, 2020

Category	Number of Countries	Population (billion)	Percent	Example
First World	59	1,440,710,000	19%	U.S., Great Britain
Second World	52	2,437,535,967	31%	China, Mexico
Third World	77	3,894,645,000	50%	Sub-Saharan Africa
Total	188	7,772,890,967	100%	

Source: World Bank Human Development Scores

The components determining rank within the index are these:

- **Life expectancy at birth**—the number of years a newborn infant could expect to live if prevailing patterns of age-specific mortality rates stay the same

- **Expected years of schooling**—number of years of schooling that a child of school entrance age can expect to receive

- **Mean years of schooling**—number of years of schooling a person 25 years of age and older

- **Gross National Income per capita**—GNI divided into the number of persons

HDI segments four strata of human advancement categories into four levels of country development: very high, high, median, and low. In this exhibit, the most glaring statistic is the GNI per Capita. The spread between the low and the high is 20 times.

10.5 Human Development Index Components, 2021

Status	HDI Average	Life Expectancy at Birth	Expected Years of Schooling	GNI Per Capita
Very High Human Development	0.881	78.7	11.9	$43,795
High Human Development	0.675	72.1	9.8	$13,232
Medium Human Development	0.624	66.8	7.1	$5,852
Low Human Development	0.484	61.0	4.3	$5,212

Source: World Bank Human Development Index

I also explored the differential from 1990-2021. Each category had differential rates of progress and through time. For instance, the "very high" category had substantial gains in the 1990-2010 period, but not much since then. Conversely, the "low human" countries had negligible movement in the 1990-2010 period and five times that in the latter period.

10.6 Human Development Index by Quality Level, 1990–2021s

Status	Number of Countries	Typical Country	1990	2010	2021	Change	
						1990–2010	2010–2021
Very High Human Development	66	U.S., United Kingdom	0.75	0.085	0.881	13.5%	3.5%
High Human Development	48	Mexico, Brazil, Indonesida	0.702	0.071	0.675	1.1%	4.9%
Medium Human Development	43	Kenya, Myanmar, Honduras	0.495	0.586	0.624	18.4%	6.5%
Low Human Development	31	Pakistan, Uganda, Ethiopia	0.452	0.444	0.484	1.8%	2.0%
Total	188						

Source: World Bank Human Development Index

In this exhibit, I pinpoint nine countries and their rank in the Human Development Index in 2000 and 2021. Notably, China has made remarkable strides in the HDI, moving from 118th nation to 79th in a 20-year period. Russia and Mexico moved up in scoring as well.

In this exhibit, all are First World countries except for Mexico and China, both of which are Second World:

10.7 Human Development Index Select Countries, 2000–2021

Country	2000		2021	
	Score	Rank	Score	Rank
Mexico	0.445	54	0.758	86
China	0.229	118	0.768	79
Russia	0.358	80	0.822	52
Germany	0.730	6	0.942	9
Canada	0.746	36	0.936	15
United States	0.728	8	0.921	21
United Kingdom	0.729	7	0.929	18
Japan	0.749	2	0.845	19
France	0.960	10	0.791	28

Source: United Nations Research

Looking at all three Second World countries noted above, several facts stand out:

- All three have had a severe reduction in fertility.

- The percent of the population under 18 years of age has declined dramatically.

- The gross domestic product (GDP) per capita has increased substantially.

Indonesia – A Classic Case

Indonesia is worth discussing because it is a Second World country that has moved up from Third World status in recent years.

The largest economy in Southeast Asia, Indonesia is a diverse archipelago nation of more than 300 ethnic groups and has charted impressive economic growth since overcoming the Asian financial crisis of the late 1990s.

Indonesia's population is approaching a quarter-billion persons. One-half of the population are on three islands: West, East, and Central Java. Jakarta, the largest city in Indonesia, is in West Java.

The **economy of Indonesia** is the largest in **Southeast Asia** and is one of the emerging market economies. As a middle-income country and member of the G20, Indonesia is classified as a **newly industrialized country**. It is the 17th largest economy in the world by nominal GDP and the seventh largest in terms of GDP per capita.

Estimated at $40 billion in 2019, Indonesia's Internet economy is expected to cross the $130 billion mark by 2025. Indonesia depends on domestic market and government budget spending and its ownership of state-owned enterprises (the central government owns 141 enterprises).

The administration of prices of a range of basic goods (including rice and electricity) also plays a significant role in Indonesia's market economy. However, since the 1990s, the majority of the economy has been controlled by individual Indonesians and foreign companies.

10.8 Indonesia

Today, **Indonesia is the world's fourth most populous nation** and 10th largest economy in terms of purchasing power parity. Furthermore, Indonesia has made enormous gains in poverty reduction, cutting the poverty rate by more than half since 1999, to under 10% in 2019 before the COVID-19 pandemic hit. Indonesia assumed the G20 presidency this year, encouraging all countries to work together to achieve a stronger and more sustainable recovery from the pandemic's impacts.

Indonesia's economic planning follows a 20-year development plan, spanning from 2005 to 2025. It is segmented into five-year, medium-term development plans called the RPJMN (*Rencana Pembangunan Jangka Menengah Nasional*), each with different development priorities. The current medium-term development plan is the last phase of the 20-year plan. It aims to further strengthen Indonesia's economy by improving the country's human capital and competitiveness in the global market.

Indonesia achieved a notable success in reducing its malnutrition rate from 37% in 2013 to under 24.4% in 2021. However, more work remains to be done to ensure strong and productive human capital development.

The World Bank's Human Capital Index revealed that the loss of learning caused by the closing down of schools during the COVID-19 pandemic will have repercussions for Indonesia's next generation.

And the sinking of Jakarta won't help matters either.

Nigeria

A Third World country that is following on the path of Indonesia is Nigeria.

Most of the Third World countries are in Africa, including sub-Saharan Africa with a population exceeding 1.0 billion people. Economic growth in sub-Saharan Africa is estimated at 2-4% annually, but far less than is needed to sustain a major population base, most of which is uneducated.

Nigeria is one of the most populous countries in the world; its rank is seventh. In Africa, it is the most populous country. Surprisingly, the

10.9 Nigeria

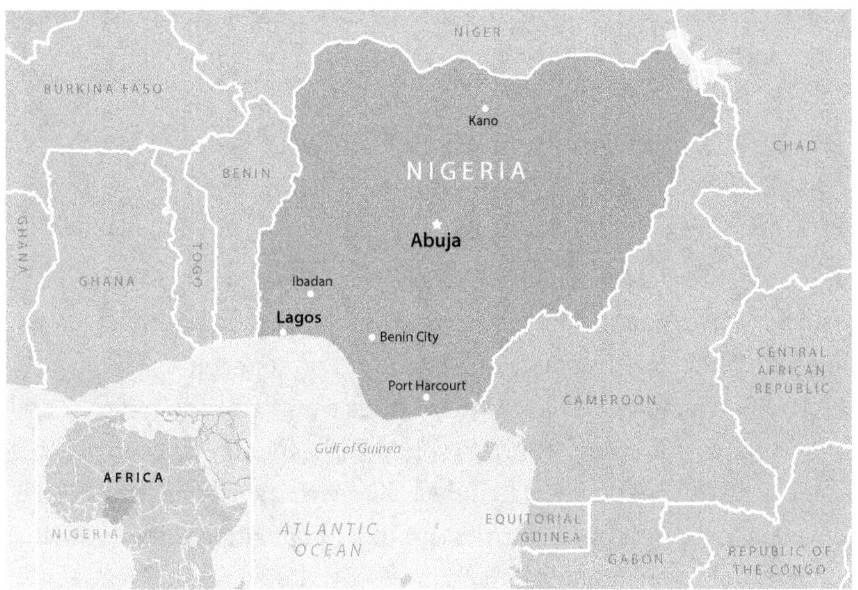

economy of Nigeria is one of the fastest growing economies of the world. Likewise, it is ranked in the "Next Eleven" economies to expand along with the member of the Commonwealth of Nations.

Moreover, the economy of the country is largely dependent upon petroleum. The other developing sectors are telecommunications and other financial services.

Nigeria's manufacturing sector is **the largest in Africa** and considered the ideal to drive Nigeria's development due to the labor-intensive, export-focused nature of manufacturing.

Its major manufacturing activities include ceramics and tiles, plastics, soaps and detergents, furniture/wood processing, and blocks and interlocking stones.

The manufacturing sector currently contributes 13 percent of Nigeria's GDP, while the government is targeting to raise it to 20per cent in 2023. Similarly, the government is also targeting to increase jobs created in the manufacturing sector from five million to six million.

Nowadays, **Nigeria is Africa's main oil producer.** With 18 operating pipelines and an average daily production of some 1.8 million barrels in

2020, Nigeria is the 11th largest oil producer worldwide. The petroleum industry accounts for about 9% of Nigeria's GDP and almost 90% of all export value.

The Key Differences Between a Third and Second World Country

There are three key elements we observe when comparing a Second and a Third World country: (1) the percent of the population that is under age 18, (2) the fertility rate, and (3) the GDP per capita.

In this example, we look at those three elements for a typical Third World country (Nigeria) and a Second World country (Indonesia). The fertility rate in Indonesia is half that of Nigeria, which leads to Nigeria having a substantially higher percent of its population under age 18.

The GDP per capita is 50% higher for Indonesia than Nigeria.

It is likely that if Nigeria continues on its current path that within two decades it could move into Second World status.

10.10 Comparison of the Economies
Indonesia and Nigeria, 2020

Factor	Indonesia	Nigeria
Status	Second World	Third World
Percent of Population Under Age 18	26.6	33.3
Fertility Rate	2.27	5.25
GDP Per Capita	**$3,855**	**$2,085**

Source: United Nations

One other indication of a country's move up in status is the percent of its population that uses the Internet. Note that in Indonesia it is 54% and in Nigeria only 36%.

Currently, 4.0 billion people have logged on to the Internet.

And that massive increase in income and education would not have happened without the advent of the computer and Internet. It is somewhat amazing to see the remarkable increase in the use of the Internet in countries that a few years ago had never seen a telephone or television.

10.11 Internet Users Selected Second and Third World Countries, 2021

Country	Percent
Viet Nam	71%
Philippines	69%
India	62%
Egypt	56%
Pakistan	56%
Indonesia	54%
Ghana	51%
Nigeria	36%
Kenya	17%
United States	**96%**

Source: World Bank

Gross Domestic Product Per Capita and Fertility Rate

GDP per capita is gross domestic product divided by midyear population. GDP is the sum of gross value added by all resident producers in the economy plus any product taxes and minus any subsidies not included in the value of the products.

It is calculated without making deductions for depreciation of fabricated assets or for depletion and degradation of natural resources. Data are in constant 2015 U.S. dollars.

Fertility rate is the number of live births for women under 45 years of age.

In exhibit 10.12, we show examples of gross domestic product per capita in the First, Second, and Third World categories and then relate it to the fertility rates in those countries.

We look at 1980, 2000, and 2021 which provides an opportunity to see how these countries have progressed over the past 30 years. As the First World countries were already mature in 1980, their progress in the last 30 years has been modest. The Second World countries have

10.12 Gross Domestic Product Per Capita
Selected First, Second, Third World Countries, 1980–2021

Country	1980	2000	2021
First World			
United States	$31,161	$48,746	$61,280
France	$23,571	$33,597	$38,210
Japan	$19,334	$31,430	$35,276
So. Korea	$4,055	$16,992	$32,644
Italy	$21,795	$21,795	$31,511
Spain	$14,727	$32,350	$26,238
Average	$19,107	$30,818	$37,527
Index	100%	161%	196%
Fertility Rate	2.02	1.54	1.35
GDP Per Fertility Rate	$9,459	$20,012	$27,797

Country	1980	2000	2021
Second World			
China	$430	$2,193	$11,188
Mexico	$7,677	$8,861	$9,255
Brazil	$6,500	$6,787	$8,551
Indonesia	$1,072	$1,867	$3,855
Viet Nam	$577	$1,170	$3,373
India	$387	$757	$1,961
	$2,774	$3,606	$6,364
	100%	130%	229%
	4.28	2.53	2.00
	$648	$1,425	$3,185

Country	1980	2000	2021
Third World			
Nigeria	$2,159	$1,450	$2,421
Cambodia	$579	$486	$1,399
Uganda	$376	$517	$894
Ethiopia	$303	$262	$852
Chad	$333	$374	$604
Somalia	$100	$200	$446
	$642	$548	$1,103
	100%	85%	172%
	6.84	6.39	4.50
	$94	$86	$245

Source: World Bank

shown major gains as have the Third World countries. In the Third World countries, their GDP per capita has almost doubled.

The exhibit also shows the impact of fertility on GDP. In particular, the Second World countries have had a severe reduction in fertility rate, thus resulting in a **five times** increase in GDP per fertility rate in that 30-year period.

In the Third World countries, the fertility rates have not declined as severely as in the Second World countries. As a result, their GDP per fertility rate has only increased **2.5 times**.

During the next half century, it is very likely that the Third World countries will gradually reduce their fertility rate.

As the fertility rates decline in those Third World countries, there will be more funds per household for consumer goods, including electronics and the Internet.

The Second World countries have almost 100% Internet availability, and some of the Third World countries have achieved 50% utilization.

What If…

What if Nigeria is able to severely reduce its fertility rate?

If it brings the fertility rate down to Indonesia's level, it is inevitable that the income per capita, and therefore spending per capita, will rise to new levels. As a result, the gross domestic product will expand dramatically. As part of that process, consumer spending will increase, health and education services will improve, and Nigeria will become part of the Second World economy.

Further, as a Second World country, it will "do business" with First World countries just as Indonesia and other Second World countries like Mexico and Brazil, thereby contributing to the overall economic growth of the world economy.

10.13 Comparison of the Economies
If Nigeria Reduces Fertility Rate to Second World Status, 2021

Factor	Indonesia	Nigeria (Current)	Nigeria
Fertility Rate	2.27	5.25	2.27
Status	Second World	Third World	**If Second World**
Percent of Population Under Age 18	26.6	33.3	26.6
Population – 2010	241,800,000	158,500,000	158,500,000
Total Population – 2021	279,134,505	211,400,000	182,909,000
Change 2010–2021	37,334,505	52,900,000	24,409,000
Percent Change	15.4%	33.4%	15.4%
Gross Domestic Product (GDP) (Billion)			
2010	$7.55	$361.50	$361.50
2021	$11.86	**$440.78**	**$567.92**
Change	$4.3	$79.28	$206.42
Percent Change	57.1%	21.9%	57.1%
Difference – Trillion			**$127.14**
Percent Difference			**260%**

Source: United Nations

Looking over the past 30 years, Indonesia has moved from a Third World country to a Second World country status with strong economic growth accompanied by reduced fertility:

10.14 Economic Growth Indonesia (Trillions), 1990–2021

Category	1990	2021	Change	Percent Change
Gross National Income Per Capita Per Capita	$1,072	$3,855	$2,783	260%
Gross Natl Income	0.531	3.471	2.94	554%

Source: World Bank

Six Challenges for Third World Countries

As I look at the next half century, I anticipate that the First and Second World countries will provide some of their resources to assist in the modernization of the Third World countries, much as the First World countries have provided substantial funds and talents to the Second World countries.

It is imperative that these Third World countries avoid going into severe debt at high interest rates in their quest to moving toward Second World status. Uncontrolled debt could be their ruination.

Even as some Third World countries have grown into success stories, most have failed to embrace true democracy, despite a hunger for it among their populations. According to Freedom House, only 11% of Africans live in countries that are considered free.

In addition to improving the basic economics of these Third World countries, there are five additional elements that are mandatory for these countries to incorporate in their move forward:

- Increasing "living wage" employment

- Improving youth education

- Achieving gender equality in the workplace

- Responding to the environmental crisis

- Bringing child labor to an end

Many countries, like Viet Nam and Bangladesh, have advanced rapidly because open global markets have allowed them to export their way to prosperity.

In her recent book *Fifty Million Rising*, author Saadia Zahidi states "that between 2000 and 2015, 50 million Muslim women joined the global workforce, raising the total to 150 million, with a combined income of $1.0 trillion."

And quoting Nobel Prize-winning economist Amartya Sen:

"A key pillar of building a multi-racial, multi-religious democracy is providing every person in every place with the prospect of a dignified life."

There are 77 Third World countries with a total of 4.0 billion people. Four billion potential consumers who will someday look forward to welcoming Amazon Prime deliveries to their homes. Today, the entire continent of Africa can't do that, although there are independent delivery services that service a few African countries.

Amazon this year will deliver **8.0 billion packages**. Better yet, almost 2.0 million small businesses sell their products through Amazon. Imagine the opportunities for small businesses in Third World countries.

It's just a matter of time and appropriate political leadership. Some countries are just luckier than others.

In 2022, President Biden and the leaders of the other G-7 countries announced that they would work with lower-income countries to invest $600 billion over the next five years as part of the Partnership for Global Infrastructure and Investment. The U.S. would contribute $200 billion toward that effort.

One hundred years ago, the rich had cars, the poor had horses. Today, the opposite is true. Things change.

CHAPTER 11

Climate Change in the United States: It's Not Going Away

Climate change is a topic that could consume all the pages in this book, but I am going to **focus on current climate change in the United States**.

Most of the climate change devastation relates to the worldwide dependence on **coal** for heating and **gas** for its vehicles. Those two fuel uses will be very difficult to eliminate, but eventually they will succumb to alternative sources. But not tomorrow. As usual, the U.S. must lead the way.

A third source of climate change is **agriculture**. According to **the United Nations Intergovernmental Panel on Climate Change**, "humans must drastically alter food production to prevent the most catastrophic effects of global warming.

"The U.N. panel of scientists looked at the climate change effects of agriculture, deforestation and other land use, such as harvesting peat and managing grasslands and wetlands. Together, those activities generate about a third of greenhouse gas emissions, including more than 40% of methane."

Currently, about **50% of the globe's vegetated land is dedicated to agriculture** and about 30% of cropland is used to grow grain for animal feed. Agriculture generates an estimated 25% of annual greenhouse gas emissions.

To keep temperatures from rising further, global greenhouse gas emissions will need to fall by 40-50% in the next decade.

A recent report by the **World Resources Institute** finds that if current dietary patterns continue, an additional 600 million hectares (1 hectare = 100 acres) would be needed to feed the projected 10 billion people in the world by 2050.

The WRI estimates that if people in the U.S. and other heavy meat-eating countries reduced their consumption of beef to about 1.5 burgers per person per week, it would nearly eliminate the need for additional agricultural expansion. Fat chance!

EVIDENCE OF CLIMATE CHANGE

The following exhibit focuses on various climatic events in five regional areas of the United States.

11.1 Evidence of Climate Change, United States

Locales	Floods	Hurricanes	Tornadoes and Cyclones	Rising Water	Rising Temperatures	Fires
South Atlantic States	X	X	X	X		
Gulf States	X	X	X	X		
MidWest			X			
Southwest					X	
Pacific States	X			X		X

In one succinct exhibit you can see the "billion dollar" climatic events in the United States from 1980 to 2022. These events have resulted in an average of 368 deaths per year and enormous costs.

11.2 "Billion Dollar" Climatic Events"
United States, 1980–2022

Type	Events	Total Costs (Billions of Dollars)	Deaths	Deaths/Year
Drought	30	$327	4,275	99
Flooding	37	$177	676	16
Freeze	9	$35	162	4
Severe Storm	163	$383	1,982	46
Tropical Cyclone	60	$1,333	6,890	160
Wildfire	21	$133	435	10
Winter Storm	21	$85	1,401	33
Total	341	$2,473	15,821	368

Source: NOAA

Hurricanes

Hurricanes seem to get the most press, mostly because as a natural disaster they are slow and big and cause substantial destruction. It is appropriate to look at the history of hurricanes in the U.S. There has been a major increase in the number of hurricanes and the number of deaths in recent decades, as noted in Exhibit 11.3.

11.3 Hurricane History, 1980–2022

Years	Billions of Losses	Number/Year	Deaths	Deaths/Year
1980–1989	$31	3.0	2,970	297
1990–1999	$55	5.5	1,062	306
2000–2009	$67	6.7	3,102	310
Avg. 1980–2009				304
2010–2019	$128	12.8	5,227	523
2020–2022	$60	20	1,400	487
2022	$18	7.9	474	474
Avg. 2010–2022				505

Source: U.S. National Climate Assessment

The most recent major U.S. hurricane was Ian in 2022. That hurricane resulted in 144 deaths, two-thirds of them people over age 65.

A hurricane's destructive force involves storm surges, which is a term for when the storm pushes the seawater higher. The rising impact of storm surges coincides with rising sea level from climate change. In the next exhibit are maps showing projected rising sea levels in 2045

11.4 Residential Properties at Risk

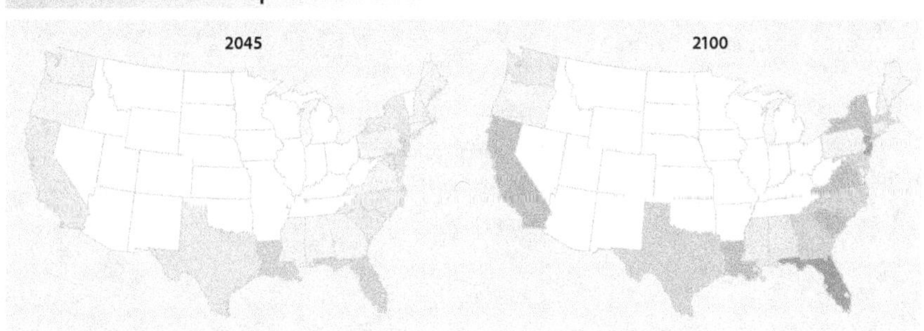

Source: ZILLOW Transaction and Assessment Dataset

and then outward to 2100. The darker the color, the more severe the rise in the water.

Based on this map, there will be almost 200 communities that can expect significant chronic flooding by 2045. Of those, 40% currently have poverty levels above the national average. The largest share is in Louisiana.

According to the *New York Times*, almost two decades after Hurricane Katrina rolled over New Orleans's Lower Ninth Ward, the population is still one-third of what it was in 2000, with only a handful of businesses to serve residents.

In May 2023, Louisiana Governor John Bel Edwards declared a state of emergency after strong winds and severe weather caused widespread power outages. More than 500,000 people were without electricity in Louisiana, Oklahoma, Arkansas, and Mississippi.

Florida holds the distinction of being the most hurricane-prone state in the country. One wonders how many newcomers to Florida will return to the wintery climates of the North after a few seasons of hurricanes.

The ability to obtain flood and hurricane insurance in Florida is proving to be difficult.

Tornadoes

The second most press-worthy climatic event is tornadoes (and/or cyclones). 2022 was a banner year for tornadoes, most of them in coastal states:

11.5 Tornadoes: Top 10 States, 2022

State	Waterfront State	Number of Tornadoes
Mississippi	X	184
Texas	X	160
Alabama	X	117
Florida	X	73
Louisiana	X	61
Georgia	X	56
Minnesota		77
Kansas		68
Arkansas		56
Iowa		53
Colorado		39

Source: National Weather Service

Exhibit 11.6 tracks the number of tornadoes from 1991 to 2022. It is rather obvious that the number of tornadoes is growing every decade.

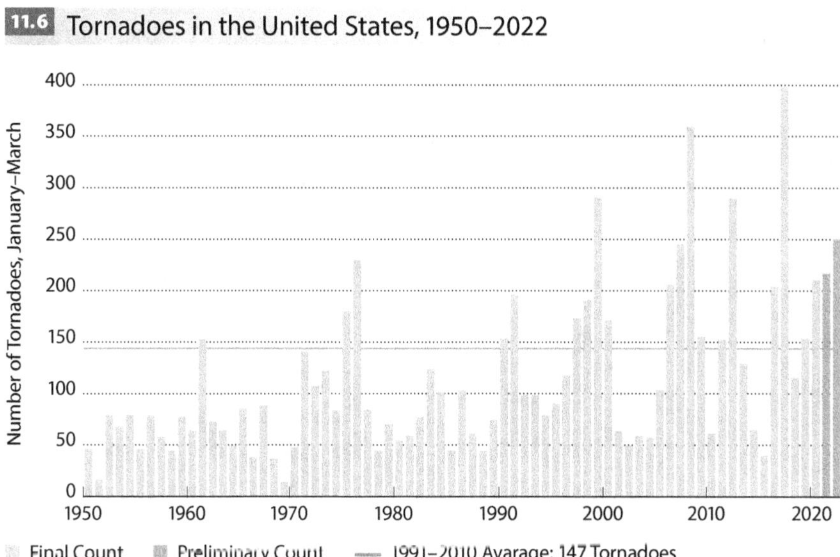

11.6 Tornadoes in the United States, 1950–2022

Source: National Oceanic and Atmospheric Administration

U.S. and Global Temperatures

In Florida, in the summer of 2023, the U.S. Weather Service issued a heat advisory, noting that the combination of high temperatures and oppressive humidity could reach between 108 and 112 degrees in places such as Key West.

In the Southwest, fire crews battled multiple wildfires in Arizona and New Mexico. Forecasters stated that triple-digit temperatures and gusty winds would lead to critical fire weather.

And, in California, wildfires in the past several years have caused rising temperatures and billions of dollars in losses.

Global temperatures have already risen about 1 degree Celsius in the past 150 years.

Wildfires

In the U.S. wildfires have typically occurred in California. Since 2003, more than 4,000,000 acres have been burned in northern and southern California, along with 9,000 structures.

11.7 The Largest Wildfires
Northern and Southern California, 2007–2021

Year	Name	Acres	Structures
Northern California			
2020	August	1,032,648	935
2021	Dixie	963,309	1,311
2018	Mendocino	459,123	280
2020	SCU Lightning	396,625	225
2020	Creek	379,895	858
Southern California			
2017	Ventura/Santa Barbara	281,898	1,080
2003	San Diego	273,246	2,820
2007	Santa Barbara	240,297	1
2007	San Diego	197,900	1,650

Source: Calfire

Of late, the Northeast states have been suffering with darkened skies and smoke, mostly coming their way from massive wildfires in Canada. Climate change is expected to result in more frequent fires in many boreal forests with severe environmental and economic consequences. Fire-prone conditions are predicted to increase across Canada as well as the U.S.

The recent wildfires in Maui which destroyed the historic town of Lahaina and killed hundreds of people are evidence of what can occur unexpectedly with climate change.

11.8 Major Wildfires in Canada, 2011–2023

Year	Name	Acres
2023	Alberta	3,000,000
2023	Nova Scotia	59,622
2019	Alberta	883,414
2018	British Columbia	3,208,550
2014	NW Territories	8,400,000
2011	Alberta	1,700,000

Source: Wikipedia

CLIMATE CHANGE AND REAL ESTATE

There are three major impacts of climate change as it relates to real estate:

- First, the **value of real estate**. One of the fundamental parts of real estate value that people in the U.S. take for granted is answering the basic question: "Is this place habitable?" Climate change-enhanced disasters physically damage and destroy buildings, and that obviously affects their value. If climate change causes those disasters to happen often enough, the answer to that question for more and more people becomes, "No."

  For example, hurricanes have destroyed values in Louisiana and on the Texas coasts and may eventually have a similar effect on other ocean and Gulf states.

- Second, the implications for the **insurance industry**.

  The insurance industry cannot be expected to cover the costs of massive climatic events, nor can property owners afford to pay the tariff that the insurance industry needs to survive. Toward that end, the federal government may be forced to be the insurer of last hope, but, if so, it will inevitably forbid development in climate change locales or mandate major changes in building codes.

  In 2023, both State Farm and Allstate announced that they will no longer write home-owner policies in California.

  In Florida, homeowners pay **four times** the national rate for insurance. Further, few of the national insurers are in the Florida market. According to CNN Business, many Florida insurers are in shaky financial shape.

- Third, there will be major changes required in the **design and development** of projects in locales with strong potential for climatic disasters. Entire new curricula are needed.

CLIMATE CHANGE CONCLUSION

It is possible to reverse the worldwide climatic patterns that have led to continuing devastation, loss of lives, and billions of dollars. It is imperative that the First World countries, and particularly the United States, lead the way.

There are 200+ million cars and trucks on the road in the U.S. and barely 3.0% are electric (or zero hydrogen). In the same vein, 3.0% of homes have solar on their roofs.

As the developing countries become more affluent, their citizens want cars and trucks. Millions of "old clunkers" (many without catalytic converters) are being sold in these countries. **Many are 15 to 20 years old and spewing effluents**.

In the U.S., if the federal government and the population are sincere in their desire to combat climate change, tax credits are a rational way to encourage installing solar panels on roofs and electrification of vehicles. Those two types of tax credits would also create an enormous increase in jobs in the two industries (as long as the manufacturing is in the U.S., of course).

Absent an aggressive anti-climatic change program worldwide, oceans will continue to rise; hurricanes, earthquakes, and tornadoes will proliferate; and trillions of dollars and a multitude of lives will be lost. We must persevere in the pursuit of solutions to addressing and mitigating climate change. We really have no choice.

CHAPTER 12

Why the U.S. Will Remain the World's Economic Driver

1. Long-term Stability and Power

The overarching reason why the U.S. will maintain world leadership is that it is a democracy with more than a century of stability. Though its politics occasionally appear unwieldy, the continuity that results from having regular elections and well-defined rules of conduct results in an orderly democracy.

Elected officials have to face the voters every few years, and therefore acceptable performance is mandatory. The two-party system with a Supreme Court inevitably results in long-term stability (even the Supreme Court changes members over time, fortunately).

Importantly, those elected most often reflect the views of the voters on a local, state, and national level.

Though we hesitate to use it, the **nation's military might** does ward off the advances of other countries. This year's DOD budget is $800 billion (including funding for Ukraine) and includes increases in benefits for the nation's 1.3 million uniformed personnel.

The budget request reflects plans for costly new defense systems—from upgrading the nation's aging nuclear weapons to developing new hypersonic weapons and new missile warning satellites.

Future intelligence agencies will have to face and conquer artificial intelligence and quantum science in order to maintain dominwance in this competitive environment.

It is worth remembering that the world has not been at war for three-quarters of a century, something I attribute to the power of the U.S. military.

Quoting Senator Elizabeth Warren: "If we do not stand up to those who seek to undermine our democracy and our economy, we will end up as bystanders to the destruction of both."

Only American power can keep the natural forces of history at bay.

2. An Educated Populace

In 1980, 50% of the jobs in America were in factory and routine clerical work. As a result of automation and globalization, these two categories now account for only 15% of American jobs.

The American economic system works because the populace has routinely increased its levels of education and training. Today, 39% of women and 36% of men have a bachelor's degree or higher. Whites and Asians have a dominance in obtaining degrees but other minorities are gradually catching up. Unlike many countries, the minorities in the U.S. have equal voting rights and relatively equal educational opportunities.

A person's chance of finishing high school soared from 6% in 1870 to 70% 100 years later.

The key is that the industries that are growing today (and paying the most) almost always require an educated workforce.

Economists segment jobs into two types: **heuristic** and **algorithmic**. The heuristic jobs require "thinking" people; the algorithmic jobs are typically blue-collar and most often involve repetitive tasks and limited education.

The continual expansion of the U.S. economy requires continual expansion of a heuristic workforce.

That is not good news for labor unions as very few of the heuristic jobs are union, but the pay scales for heuristic jobs are definitely bullish.

As increasing percentages of voters achieve college degrees, there will be a noticeable swing in voting patterns more often toward liberal policies. As heuristic workers have to think for themselves, that has spilled over into their political behavior.

Having a large middle class is critical for fostering good government. And it increases the demand for domestic goods and services and helps fuel consumption-led growth.

Unfortunately, in a survey of high school students by the Society of Woman Engineers, only 6.0% of young women express an interest in having a career in science and engineering, compared to 15% of males. Numerous school districts are adding STEM courses to entice male and female students into the sciences.

Notably, women have been able to take their place in Congress and in state offices. Women hold close to 25% of the House of Representatives and Senate.

3. Demographics

Every year of late our population expands by more than two million, and we now have more than 330 million people in our nation.

The demographics of the U.S. are an interesting mix of native-born and foreign-born. Today, one-quarter of the population is foreign-born. Those who are foreign-born are often in the U.S. because they have escaped countries that are not democratic and often ruled by tyrants.

Further, many of the foreign-born are educated people and can immediately contribute to the economies of their community and their professions. One-third have a bachelor's or graduate degree.

Of the 104 Americans who have been awarded Nobel Prizes in chemistry, medicine, and physics, 40 have been immigrants.

Each year we admit more than 1.0 million persons to the U.S., thus allowing for population growth despite the continuing decline in birthrates.

Nearly 50 million people immigrated to the U.S. from 1950 to 2015.

As noted in the chapter on aging, it is imperative that in order to have a routinely growing economy, we must have routinely growing population. The two go hand in hand. The U.S. needs to grow by 3.0+

million persons annually in order to achieve economic growth rates that parallel the past.

And it is totally normal for the U.S. to have a substantial number of illegal entrants. It's always been that way. And they account for a large part of our entry-level labor force.

As New York's Consolidated Edison has long noted, "And grow we must."

4. English Language

It is also important that English is a comparatively easy language to learn and most immigrants have a good knowledge of the language before arriving in the U.S. In most First and Second World countries, English is taught in grade schools. And, of course, it is the native language of multiple nations around the world including the U.S., Australia, Great Britain, et al.

Countries like Japan, South Korea, China, and Russia would dearly love to have substantial immigration, but their language, both written and spoken, is a barrier that is severe to overcome. In many of the countries discussed in this book, their populations are on a downhill course due to out-migration and families that hesitate to have more than one child.

In the same vein, in most countries it is far more difficult for women to achieve employment, salaries, and benefits on par with men.

Berlitz can provide a newcomer with passable English in 60 days (concentrated). Not so with most other foreign tongues. And learning how to write in those tongues could take a year or so to master. And the problem with learning a language like Japanese or Chinese is that it is not transferable to other countries.

5. Home Ownership Percentage

A great part of the economic and governmental stability of this nation results from home ownership. In most states, more than two-thirds of households own their own home. (Unfortunately, California home ownership is a constant and disappointing 50%.)

Nationwide, that level of home ownership stability has been a constant for more than a half century. Of equal importance, 83% of married couples own their home.

In many countries, China and Russia for instance, homeowners do not own the land under their homes. And in many countries, loan-to-value ratios on home loans (if they exist at all) are far less than in the U.S.

On the West Coast, as much as one-third of the home ownership in the U.S. is foreign-born. In the San Jose metropolitan area, 45% of home ownership is foreign-born.

Also, unlike many (maybe most) countries, home loans are relatively easy to obtain in the U.S. and are very often at very favorable loan-to-value percentages, regardless of race, creed, or religion.

6. Dual Incomes

Unlike some countries, women in the U.S. are educated and welcomed into the workforce. As a result, dual incomes are typically sufficiently high to allow a couple to own a home, drive one or two cars, and have a child or two. Unfortunately, women are still not paid on an equal basis with men in many industries, but they are slowly catching up.

According to Pew Research, in 49% of marriages in 1972 the husband was the sole breadwinner. Today that figure is 23%. Today, in 29% of dual-job marriages, the wife earns the same as the husband.

In the U.S., two-thirds of married women have a job. The higher the level of education, the higher the percent with a job.

Some other countries are improving access to healthcare and women's access to education. The U.S. fosters those countries that are recognizing women's rights.

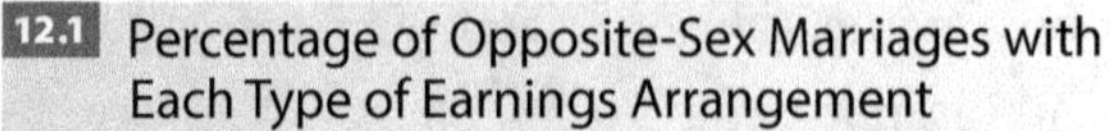

Percentage of Opposite-Sex Marriages with Each Type of Earnings Arrangement

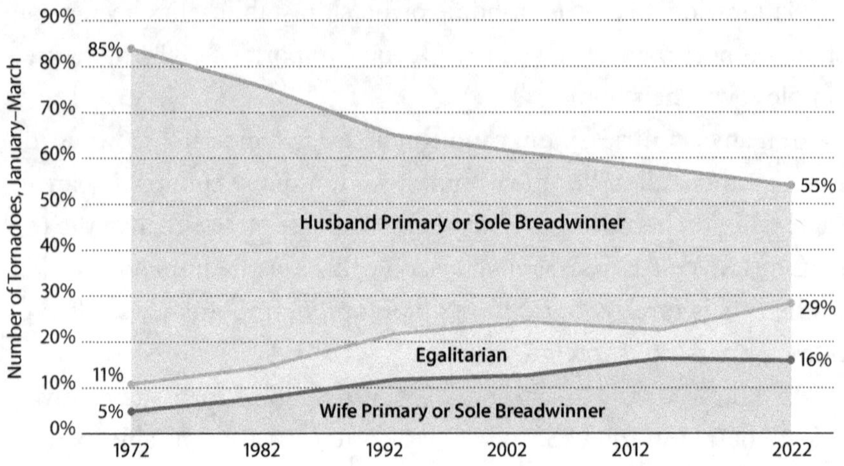

7. Net Worth

Net worth is a concept that is foreign to most countries, as is the ability to pass on that net worth to future generations. Further, few countries have pension funds or IRAs or 401ks.

In most Second World and Third World countries, an inheritance is meager. Life insurance is a great unknown in most Second and Third World countries. As a result, the children in those countries have little chance of accumulating capital when their parents pass away.

The inability to save money typically means that funds are not available to pay for college, therefore resulting in a populace that can't assist countries in those industries that require education as well as brainpower.

Having net worth also provides a level of confidence. Facing starvation on a regular basis does not lead to a lifestyle of confidence and experimentation.

According to wealth manager United Income Inc., over the next 30 years $36 trillion will flow from one generation to the next in the United States. Americans inherited $427 billion in 2016 (latest data available). Our children will live well.

8. International Investment and Capitalism

Stable capitalist countries are able to attract international investment, thereby creating an environment that allows scientific, educational, and research firms to raise billions in venture capital and also invest in real estate.

Foreign direct investment in the United States in 2021 was $4.9 trillion. Almost half was invested in manufacturing. The two countries with the largest investments in the U.S. are Japan and Germany.

Capitalism has been quite successful as a system of political economy, especially when the alternative is socialism. Capitalism took off in the 19th century and has dominated economic growth ever since. Most importantly, it has lifted hundreds of millions of people out of poverty and will continue to do so throughout this century.

Capitalism is here to stay and has no competitors. Competition within the capitalistic system will shape the future of the global economy. Obviously, a country like China has its own brand of capitalism, but it is capitalism nonetheless.

Our strategy: commit to the defense of countries that share U.S. values or interests by expanding trade, upholding rules-based institutions, and fostering liberal values internationally.

The only path forward is for countries to jointly manage the flow of goods, capital, and people.

9. Workplace Flexibility

Thanks to COVID, there are immense changes taking place in our workplace habits. The flexibility of enterprise owners will result in a long-term change in where and how we work. This flexibility has occurred amazingly rapidly and apparently with minimal change in workplace efficiency and output.

There will be major changes in office space demand with a multitude of studies that will drill down into how office workers move up the management scale when they never see their bosses except on Zoom or Teams. Will personalities no longer be a factor in promotions? Can you stay home and let AI write your reports?

And, of course, what will become of the millions of square feet of office space that is permanently vacant? Will it all be converted to apartments? Or, maybe scrapped?

And will every new home have an office or maybe lab space?

10. Scientific Advancement

The U.S. has been the world leader in pharmaceutical and medical research. In the past few decades, the incidence of polio has decreased by 99% worldwide. There have also been major advances in diagnostics, organ replacement, and general surgery.

Science has led to major cures for malaria, a disease that affects some 200 million people annually, some 450,000 of them dying from the disease. The Gates Foundation has played a major role in the demise of malaria.

In the same vein, there have been major advances in nutrition and genomic research, including the dramatic climb in agricultural productivity, gene editing, and genetic engineering. Gene editing has been identified as a source of disease treatment including certain cancers, muscular dystrophy, Lyme disease, and sickle cell anemia.

The U.S. has pioneered the development of CRISPR ("clustered regularly interspaced short palindromic repeats"), which is a method for editing DNA far more precisely and efficiently than was possible with older technologies. It will revolutionize gene editing.

11. Geography

Author Peter Zeihan often states that the greatness of America is abetted by the fact that it has oceans to the east and west and one country in the north and one in the south and both of which are friendly. That situation allows Americans to have a long-term confidence in their stability knowing that attacks to the mainland are not probable.

12. Educational and Vocational Advancement

Finally, the U.S. is a nation wherein educational and vocational advancement is available to everyone. It is not based on who your parents are or where you were born or what your religion is. It is my thesis that only a person's unwillingness to go the extra mile will keep them from success.

In most communities, community colleges offer highly usable knowledge in a myriad of vocations (at minimal cost) and, in most states, a community college degree can lead to a bachelor's degree or higher. And, of course, there remain well-paying jobs in many industries that do not require college degrees. Certainly construction is one of them.

All these factors taken together lead me to the conclusion that the U.S. will continue to be the leader of the free and not so free world. And it is the obligation of the U.S. to aid and abet the advancement of countries that need a helping hand in their quest to join the ranks of the educated and affluent.

And in the words of President Theodore Roosevelt:

"Much has been given us, and much will rightfully be expected from us. We have become a great nation, forced by the fact of its greatness into relations with other nations of the earth, and we must behave as beseems a people with such responsibilities."

INDEX

Acknowledgments

I had the good fortune to work with a skilled publishing team and with a number of professionals who reviewed various chapters. Thank you to each of you for your valuable contributions to this book.

Professional Team:

- Martha Bullen, Publishing consultant, Bullen Publishing Services
- Christy Day, Constellation Book Services
- David Aretha, Editor
- David Ruppe, Graphic designer
- Amy Murphy, Indexing

Talented Professionals:

Jan Sachs, founder of an advertising agency in Chicago and a commercial Realtor in San Diego County, reviewed and edited many of the chapters.

Phillip Adams, a marketing guru and editor of great merit, reviewed several chapters.

Ken Singh, an attorney formerly based in India, reviewed the chapter on India.

A.J. Hatkar, founder of the ARCAids consulting firm in Mumbai and a founder of the India chapter of Lambda Alpha International, reviewed the chapter on India.

Fiam Gershman, senior research engineer, Solar Turbines, and immigrant to the United States from USSR, reviewed the chapter on Russia.

Rene Smith, retired naval commander, reviewed and edited the first and last chapter.

Professor Maxwell McCombs, retired chair of the Journalism Department at the University of Texas, reviewed the section on Texas.

Holly Elmore, CEO of Elemental Impact, reviewed the chapter on the South Atlantic states and Climate Change.

Dr. Steven Altman, former president, University of Central Florida, reviewed the chapter on the South Atlantic states.

Dr. Mitra Kanaani, FAIA, former chair, Undergraduate Program, New School of Architecture and Design, reviewed the chapters on the European Union and Climate Change.

Professor John Demas, LLB, Knauss School of Business, University of San Diego, reviewed Chapter 1.

Mark Goldman, finance professor, San Diego State University, reviewed the Chapter 2.

Jon Nevin, a frequent India visitor, reviewed the chapter on India.

About the Author

 **Alan Nevin** is a real estate economist, demographer, and futurist.

He is the director of the Economic Research Division of GAFCON, a nationwide construction management consulting firm based in San Diego.

His consulting practice concentrates on providing advice for real estate owners and developers, and he serves the legal community as an expert witness in real estate related litigation and as an appraiser.

Prior to joining GAFCON, Alan was a principal at London Moeder Real Estate Advisors, and before that was director of Research for 14 years with MarketPointe Realty Advisors. In the past, he served as director of Real Estate Research for HomeFed Bank and was president of ConAm Securities, a subsidiary of ConAm Management Company.

His first book, *The Great Divide*, analyzes the demographic patterns that shape the world and the United States in particular over the next quarter century.

Alan earned a Master of Arts degree in Statistical Research from Stanford University, a Bachelor of Arts degree in Marketing and a Master of Business Administration in Real Estate Economics from American University in Washington, D.C.

He is a co-founder of the UC San Diego Economics Roundtable, a member of the Advisory Board of the UC San Diego Real Estate and Development Program, an elected Fellow of the Lambda Alpha International Land Economics Society, and an active member of the Land Economics Foundation.

To learn more or contact Alan, please visit www.nevinadvisors.com.